What Others Are Saying

With her trademark honesty, warmth, wit, and humor, Kathy inspires us to grin with joy, regardless of our circumstances. But she doesn't stop there. I love how every chapter of *The Grin Gal's Guide to Joy* also encourages us to grow with joy, go with joy, and give with joy. This study challenges readers to apply the truths we've learned immediately in our everyday lives and then share them with others."

—CHRISTIN DITCHFIELD, internationally syndicated radio host, conference speaker, and author of over 80 books, including *What Women Should Know About Letting It Go*

Kathy Carlton Willis writes stories from her open-book life in a way that makes me want to say, "She gets me! She really really *gets* me!" Because of her humorous outlook and honest confessions, I want to take a deeper look at how God's joy works in and through me. If you've ever wished you could grin with joy despite overwhelming circumstances, this book is for you. I can highly recommend *The Grin Gal's Guide to Joy* for your own reading, or for a group setting.

—PAT LAYTON, author, *Life Unstuck*

How can a Bible study be simultaneously so thorough, so meaty, so thought provoking, and so entertaining? I'm not sure how Kathy pulled it off, but *The Grin Gal's Guide to Joy* is all those things and more. You'll relate to the concepts whether you're just starting your joy journey or are a seasoned traveler. Pick up this book if you want to be inspired not only to find more joy, but to create more joy in the lives of others.

—DR. THELMA WELLS (MAMA T), speaker, author, *A Woman of God Ministries*

The Grin Gal's Guide to Joy had me giggling and nodding my head in commiseration. With truth and transparency, Kathy Carlton Willis strips off the layers and gets right to the heart of the matter of choosing a joy-filled life. Like trying on swimsuits after a long, calorie-laden winter, Kathy grins and bares her soul in a way that reminds us that joy isn't found in perfect circumstances, but in a perfect Christ. I highly recommend this study for everyone who longs for more laughter in their lives and more serenity in their spirits.

—RENAE BRUMBAUGH GREEN, ECPA bestselling author and award-winning humor columnist

In trial and triumph, sorrow and celebration, joy is the Christian's constant companion. Kathy captures this truth beautifully in *The Grin Gal's Guide to Joy*. Using humor, transparent stories and solid biblical studies, she shows how Jesus splashes his supernatural, abundant joy into our messy lives, and how the overflow of his joy can heal and transform others. Joy is surely the Spirit's work within us, but it's also our choice. What a practical, insightful and motivating book!

—DAWN WILSON, founder of Heart Choices Today, upgradewithdawn.com

Is your life missing the joy God promised? Kathy Carlton Willis shows you how to experience it in her new book *The Grin Gal's Guide to Joy*. This unique book is a delightful blend of heartwarming stories, Bible study, and practical, hands-on life application. Kathy is humorously serious about joy! She doesn't just tell us why we can grin with joy, she shows us how to go out and live joyfully.

—**Kathy Howard, speaker, Bible teacher and author of 8 Bible studies and devotionals**

I was amazed at how many "joy" Scriptures Kathy Carlton Willis unveils from the Bible! You'll have no doubt after reading *The Grin Gal's Guide to Joy*, that God wants us all living joy-filled lives. With Kathy's trademark humor, personal stories, thought-provoking questions, prodding, and mentoring, you'll find yourself wanting to grin and shout for joy no matter what your circumstances. You'll relate to the concepts in this Bible study, wherever you are in your joy journey. Pick up this book if you want more joy of the Lord in your life, and then joyfully "serve it forward" to others.

—**Janet Thompson, Woman to Woman Mentoring, speaker and author of 20 books including** *Everyday Brave: Living Courageously As a Woman of Faith*

Paul exhorts us to "rejoice in the Lord always." How is that one working out for you? Joy can be illusive when we are focused on our circumstances. *The Grin Gal's Guide to Joy* gives the solution: directing our gaze toward God, the true source and provider of joy. With relatable stories of finding joy even in the challenges of life, Kathy Carlton Willis leads the way with wonderful humor and refreshing honesty. Her joy is infectious! Get ready to grin with joy!

—**Julie Zine Coleman, speaker and author, managing editor for Arise Daily (Advanced Writers and Speakers Assoc.) juliecoleman.org**

The Grin Gal's Guide to Joy addresses the prickly places of life in a positive way, yet it doesn't gloss over reality. I enjoyed Kathy's stories, humor, and practical tips, but most of all, I appreciated her ability to touch my soul and soothe it with meaningful spiritual application. If you need a joy boost, then start smiling, because *The Grin Gal's Guide to Joy* will provide and surprise.

—**Anita Agers Brooks, inspirational business/life coach, international speaker, and award-winning author of** *Getting Through What You Can't Get Over*

The Grin Gal's Guide to Joy will be my go-to resource when I find myself slipping out of God's best and settling for a humdrum lifestyle. Kathy Carlton Willis put together a practical roadmap to joy with an easy blend of Bible word studies, comical and heartwarming stories and how-to tips. Joy naturally spills out of those carrying it onto those around them. *The Grin Gal's Guide to Joy* points the way to your next fill-up.

—BETH PATCH, **Spiritual Life Editor for CBN.com**

Kathy Carlton Willis admits she seems to accumulate trials like valuable collectibles. Boy, can I relate! Can you? We might ask how it's possible to operate out of a mindset of joy when the not-so-fun stuff of life hits us from every side. The good news is that in *The Grin Gal's Guide to Joy*, Kathy walks alongside us, encouraging us on our faith journey. Using experiential wisdom, plenty of Scripture, and a nice blend of humor and transparency, she shows us that yes, indeed, joy can be a reality in our lives. Whether studying her book alone or in a group setting, you—and the people around you—will be encouraged and blessed.

—TWILA BELK, **a writer and speaker who loves braggin' on God. Author of** *The Power to Be: Be Still, Be Grateful, Be Strong, Be Courageous* **and seven other titles**

The Grin Gal's Guide to Joy is one of the most relevant studies I've read on the topic of joy. I was really drawn in by Kathy's personal stories. They opened up my eyes, ears and heart to be more receptive to what the Bible says about joy. Kathy doesn't merely share stories for the sake of entertainment, but she ties them into Scripture in a way that challenges me to want to deliver more joy to others.

—LYNDA T. YOUNG, **author of the** *You Are Not Alone* **Book series,** *Hope for Families of Children with Cancer,* **and** *Hope for Families of Children on the Autistic Spectrum*

I was so excited to read another of Kathy's books. Kathy always produces books chockfull of information, and *The Grin Gal's Guide to Joy* is no exception. With an insightful blend of biblical and practical principles, Kathy teaches us to respond with joy in the face of difficult circumstances. A must read for anyone who needs a little more joy in their lives.

—MICHELLE S. LAZUREK, **Two-time award winner of the children's book of the year award for** *Daddy am I beautiful?* **and** *Uniquely You*

The GRIN GAL'S GUIDE TO Joy

A Story, Study & Steps 7-Week Bible Study

Kathy Carlton Willis

3G BOOKS

The Grin Gal's Guide to Joy
©2020 by Kathy Carlton Willis
www.kathycarltonwillis.com

ISBN-13: 978-1-7330728-1-6

Published by 3G Books, Beaumont, TX 77706
www.threegbooks.com

All rights reserved. No part of this book may be reproduced, stored in a retrieval system, or transmitted in any form or by any means – electronic, mechanical, photocopy, recording, or otherwise – without written permission of the publisher, except for brief quotations in printed reviews.

Unless otherwise noted, Scripture quotations are taken from the Holy Bible, New Living Translation, copyright ©1996, 2004, 2007 by Tyndale House Foundation. Used by permission of Tyndale House Publishers, a Division of Tyndale House Ministries, Carol Stream, Illinois 60188. All rights reserved.

Scripture quotations marked ESV are from The ESV® Bible (The Holy Bible, English Standard Version®), copyright © 2001 by Crossway, a publishing ministry of Good News Publishers. Used by permission. All rights reserved.

Scriptures marked KJV are taken from the King James Version, public domain.

Scripture quotations marked MSG are taken from *THE MESSAGE*, copyright © 1993, 2002, 2018 by Eugene H. Peterson. Used by permission of NavPress. All rights reserved. Represented by Tyndale House Publishers, a Division of Tyndale House Ministries.

Scriptures marked NKJV are taken from the New King James Version®. Copyright © 1982 by Thomas Nelson. Used by permission. All rights reserved.

Scripture quotations taken from the Amplified® Bible (AMP),
Copyright © 2015 by The Lockman Foundation
Used by permission. www.Lockman.org

Edited by Robin Steinweg and Rick Steele
Copyedited by Diane Stortz
Proofread by Leisa Stokes

Interior and Cover Design by Michelle Rayburn
www.missionandmedia.com

CONTENTS

Group Study Schedule... xi

Introduction: What Does It Mean to Grin with Joy?................. xiii

Learn Kathy's background, why she wrote this book, and how the study is set up.

1 The Joy of Direction and Obedience 1

God's Word directs us and reveals his will. He gives us discernment to know how to follow him, and when we obey him, we experience great joy. Even though it's difficult to explain, we discover a deeper level of joy as we give up our lives to live for him.

2 The Works of Joy 13

God's Word and God's Spirit work in us—we are all works in progress. We in turn produce fruit pleasing to him. Good works are not necessary for salvation, but they are evidence of a life dedicated to Christ. When we operate from hearts of service, we experience joyful enthusiasm and a spirit of gratitude.

3   The Joy of the Gospel 25

When Christ began his work on earth, it brought God the Father great joy. Pleasing the Father brought Jesus Christ joy. And the gospel delivers joy to each believer who receives the gift of the good news.

4   The Celebration of Joy 35

We have reason to celebrate as we receive the blessings bestowed to us from the Father. He has done amazing things—what good news! We place our trust in him and experience joyful gladness. We can be of good cheer when we commemorate his work.

5   The Joy of Correction and Forgiveness 47

Because God loves us, he corrects us. There is joy even in his discipline, as we see his hand on our lives. As we accept his forgiveness and extend forgiveness to others, guilt is cleared and joy flourishes. We rejoice as sin is wiped clean and relationships are restored.

6   The Joy of Refuge and Renewal 57

God provides us with the safety of his refuge. He ransoms us with the sacrifice of his Son. And he renews us to live fully in him. We rejoice as we savor his goodness. Our joy is elevated to new heights as we experience his unfailing love.

7   The Joy of Wisdom 67

God gives his children the ability to process knowledge through discernment, which results in great wisdom. As we gain his insights, our joy increases. And when we make choices based on his wisdom, we please God. Our joy grows as he delights in us.

8   The Fullness of Joy 75

As the joy of the Lord fills us, we are moved to worship him, surrendered completely. This joy increases as we focus on his attributes and good works. In the presence of his majesty, we experience the awe of joyful adoration.

9 The Songs of Joy 87

The Lord's goodness leads us to worship him in song. Our posture acknowledges his lordship, and our mouths praise his name. We shout for joy as we seek his face and experience his blessings. Music fills the air and joy fills each heart.

10 The Endurance of Joy 103

Even in tremendous trials we can experience great joy because we abide in Christ. He equips us to endure hardship and to wait patiently for his good endings. We anticipate answered prayers while we continue to joyfully seek and serve him.

11 The Tears of Joy 115

We experience joy even when weeping, in the midst of suffering and mourning, knowing the blessing of God's presence in our lives. God inspires rejoicing despite the grief. Only in him can we surrender our anguish and experience a joy that humanly doesn't make sense.

12 The Benefits of Joy 125

The Lord gives us blessings as we seek him. We embrace his good gifts and rejoice with thanksgiving. We delight in the results of placing our lives in his hands. It is our joy to see his amazing works through us and to us on this faith journey.

13 The Abundance of Joy 139

Just as we enjoy abundant life in Christ, we also delight in the abundance of his joy. It fills us and overflows from us. The supply of his joy never runs out. All creation bursts forth in joyful praise.

Conclusion 149
Leader's Guide 151
Acknowledgments 167
About the Author 169

GROUP STUDY SCHEDULE

This Bible study can be used by individuals or groups. If you are reading on your own, feel free to take your time, going at your own pace—absorb and implement as many of these ideas as possible.

If you are doing this study with a group, the suggested schedule below covers two or three chapters in the book each week—enough material for a consistent pace for a seven-week group study. If you want more time together, simply divide the chapters into a schedule that works for your group. Use or adapt the group plans in the Leader's Guide at the back of the book with whatever schedule you choose.

Week One

Introduction: What Does It Mean to Grin with Joy?

Week Two: His Word Brings Joy

1   The Joy of Direction and Obedience

2   The Works of Joy

Week Three: Good News Brings Joy

3 The Joy of the Gospel

4 The Celebration of Joy

Week Four: God Brings Joy

5 The Joy of Correction and Forgiveness

6 The Joy of Refuge and Renewal

7 The Joy of Wisdom

Week Five: Worship Brings Joy

8 The Fullness of Joy

9 The Songs of Joy

Week Six: Trials Bring Joy

10 The Endurance of Joy

11 The Tears of Joy

Week Seven: Blessings Bring Joy

12 The Benefits of Joy

13 The Abundance of Joy

INTRODUCTION

What Does It Mean to Grin with Joy?

Sometimes in life we simply need to grin with joy. This study examines the word *joy* in Scripture. It will equip you with the tools to experience and extend God's abundant and overflowing joy. Since life is more bearable with laughter, humorous transparency is woven into each chapter. Hence, *The Grin Gal's Guide to Joy*.

When I ponder what it means to grin with joy, I think of the joy of friendship. I smile every time I recall my childhood friend Patricia. Read on to discover how bursts of joy bubbled up through the years of our friendship.

Purple Patty

On tippy-toes, I picked up the handset of the black, rotary-dial wall phone. Dialing just five numbers, I reached my best friend, next-door neighbor Patty Rubemeyer. "Hi, Patty! What did Santa bring you this Christmas?"

"He brought me a doll bed and a teddy bear and a . . . and a . . ."

Every year we called each other when gift opening was complete. On Christmas Day, we never walked across the alley to talk because chatting over the phone like grown-ups was half the fun. Often our parents compared Christmas lists when deciding what Santa should bring. One year Patty received the walking version of a doll, and I received the talking version. We believed they were twins!

THE GRIN GAL'S GUIDE TO JOY

On Christmas Day 1968, we both found sewing kits under our trees. Not knowing what a needle threader was, I threw away what I believed to be the *label*. Later, Mrs. Rubemeyer kidded me about my poochy lip when I pouted about the missing threader. I wanted my sewing kit to be just like Patty's!

Patty and I did everything together. We walked to school together. We played together. And when called for, we were even disciplined together. It was not unusual to see Patty's nose pointed in one corner of the room and mine in another as our mothers grew impatient with our antics.

Patty taught me many lessons. She told me the secret of Santa and the facts of life. There wasn't much we didn't share. Even after we no longer believed in Santa, Patty and I called every Christmas of our childhood to talk about our gifts.

Phone calls changed as we approached adolescence. We chatted about friends and activities. A friend of her brother teasingly declared Patty "the monster from the purple lagoon." She was no monster. Purple appropriately wrapped up the color of Patty's personality, so the name stuck. My best friend Patty became my best friend Purple.

"What are you wearing to the Christmas party tonight?" I asked Purple.

"T-shirt and blue jeans. What else?"

"I was thinking of dressing up a little bit. This guy might be the one," I whispered into the phone. I didn't want to jinx my luck by saying it too loudly.

Purple made high school fun. She was a year older and helped me fit in. We sang in choir and musicals, and worked hard to create the school newspaper and yearbook. We even received honors as the only charter members in our school's Quill and Scroll Society.

As we matured, we began to get serious about our futures. Our boyfriends soon became our fiancées, and we planned a joint engagement party for when else—the Christmas season! It was fun to act the part of soon-to-be wives as we planned the menu, cooked the meal, and decorated the dining room for guests. Soon after the party, Purple's engagement was called off, but my wedding plans continued.

"Purple, will you be my maid-of-honor?"

"Of course!" she replied. "I would be mad if you asked anyone else."

What a friend! Even though we weren't planning our weddings together, she put her own life aside to be the maid of honor rather than the bride.

INTRODUCTION

On our one-year wedding anniversary, my husband and I gathered with friends for a reunion. Purple met me at a restaurant before the reunion so we could squeeze in some girl talk.

"Kathy, you've put on a few pounds. Obviously, marriage agrees with you."

I just beamed. Only a best friend could tease me about gaining weight and get by with it! Giddy with catching up, we easily picked up where we had left off. Friendships like this are destined to last a lifetime.

Many years passed without our traditional Christmas phone call. I sent out my annual Christmas newsletter to friends and family. Purple was on my mailing list, even though her name and address had changed. One year while I hung Christmas decorations, the phone rang. As I teetered on a chair to place an ornament near the back of the tree, Russ answered the phone.

"Why, yes! Kathy would welcome an interruption from you!"

Sensing the importance of this call, I hopped down from the chair to pick up the phone. I heard a polished voice say, "Hi, Kathy. This is Patricia. Do you remember me?"

Of course I remembered her! My kid friend Patty, and my teen friend Purple, was now my adult friend Patricia. Once again, we picked up our conversation right where we had left off. We talked about her new husband and my new ministry. We caught up on all the family gossip and then promised to stay in touch.

A few years later, I flew across several states to speak at a Christmas tea ten miles from my hometown. I scanned the group for familiar faces as I shared Christmas memories. When I told about my Christmas calls with Patricia, I discovered her eyes gleaming back at me from the audience.

> Not even death can separate friends when we can pick up right where we left off one day in heaven.

Imagine my joy as her presence made my holiday complete! I hustled to her table as soon as I finished speaking. Our friendship had endured twenty years of being apart.

Even though she is gone now, I grin when I think of our friendship. Not even death can separate friends when we can pick up right where we left off one day in heaven. Until then, I grin with joy from the memories we made!

How Chapters Are Structured

The Grin Gal's Guide to Joy will capture some of the joy-filled moments in our lives and provide Bible instruction for spiritual growth on the subject as well. Sort of like *Chicken Soup* meets Bible word studies and then collides with a how-to manual!

Each chapter includes the following sections:

- **Grin with Joy** contains real-life stories and observations that will cause you to smile. You'll laugh at the humorous confessions and wacky insights and relate to the transparent honesty. And you'll be inspired to rejoice in your everyday situations.

- **Grow with Joy** is our Bible study. We'll dissect verses and see what they mean to us personally. I'll share my thoughts, and you'll have journal space to write down your thoughts as well. The best way to process Scripture is to make it personal.

- **Go with Joy** offers life-application steps for the concepts we've just discussed. This is where you get suggestions for putting our lesson into action. Pick one idea and make it work for you, or pick them all—but do something to live out your faith with joy.

- **Give with Joy** takes life application one step further; we grab what we've learned and give it away to others. This is when faith becomes ministry; when our focus expands to see the needs of someone else. Each of us can extend the joy of the Lord to others. In this section we have an opportunity to serve it forward.

- **Your Grin-with-Joy Challenge** describes a joy-challenging scenario to give you an opportunity to exercise your newfound perspective on joy. It allows for speculation and judgment calls to prepare you for the what-ifs that happen in life *before* they happen. Even if you never experience the exact scenario, by thinking through these challenges you can evaluate and make adjustments to your typical responses to make sure they are filled with joy. These challenges are also a good way to consider advice you might give friends going through something similar.

Grin Gal Pals

Consider selecting a Grin Gal Pal while going through this study. Together you can encourage and pray for each other and have an accountability partner for any of the action steps you decide to take as you grin, grow, go and give with joy. The more transparent you are with your Grin Gal Pal time, the more you'll see joy in your everyday lives.

INTRODUCTION

Just Grin with Joy When . . .

Since I love when my readers laugh along with me, here's a "Just Grin with Joy When . . ." list to kick-start your funny bone. *(If it wasn't for an abundance of joy already residing in my heart, I would not have been able to grin with joy during the following exchanges. You may laugh, but these all happened to me during the writing of this book.)*

- The hair stylist asks if you've considered doing something about your facial hair. Um—I thought I took care of those pesky hairs before I left home. Maybe I'm going blind. *Grin.*

- A well-meaning article review comes in, attacking your transparency about changing churches, suggesting you should be more dedicated to the Lord's service. The writer didn't know about my more than thirty years in church ministry. Should I reply to the criticism? *Grin* and bear it.

- A ministry team suggests your sweet voice keeps them from being upset when you have to say hard things to hold them accountable at a planning meeting. *Grin* and bat eyelashes.

- A dignified individual gives you "the look" when you and a friend share a belly laugh. *Grin* and guffaw harder.

- You tell your husband he must not have looked hard enough for that certain product at the grocery store. Then you find out it's been discontinued. *Grin* and apologize.

- You move heaven and earth to set aside time to spend with someone. They no-show for a lunch date at their own house with no apology! *Grin* with joy (through slightly clenched teeth).

- In the restaurant restroom, the toilet seat pinches the sensitive skin of your inner thigh, and you realize it isn't as painful as the awkward conversation you've just had with guests at the table. *Grin* and return to the table with a slight waddle.

- You're asked for the millionth time about being childless. You explain you're still getting to know each other. She knows you've been married more than thirty years. *Grin* and leave her scratching her head.

Chapter One

THE *Joy* OF DIRECTION AND OBEDIENCE

The Lord gives his people perpetual joy when they walk in obedience to him. —**D.L. Moody**

God's Word directs us and reveals his will. He gives us discernment to know how to follow him, and when we obey him, we experience great joy. Even though it's difficult to explain, we discover a deeper level of joy as we give up our lives to live for him.

Grin with Joy

The funniest thing happened yesterday. I had arranged for two volunteers and a staff person to go to a residence to pick up some donations. None of the three could find it and assumed I had written down the wrong address. After calling the residence, they discovered I had given them the right address after all, so they got a description of the house and tried again. The house number was supposed to be 703, but they found the home at 803. The homeowner still swore the address was 703 even though one of my volunteers found the 803 on the house! Did the homeowner really know where he was?

Many couples on road trips end up arguing because the navigator cannot read the road map or directions fast enough for the driver to know which way to turn. Often the driver doesn't ask the passenger to help navigate until it's too late. Did the driver really know where he was?

When I was a child, a teacher once placed me on the wrong bus after school. None of the surroundings looked familiar. The students had different faces. The bus driver was a different man. The streets had different houses. I didn't know where I was!

In life there will be times when we feel as if we don't know where we are. We rush through life at such a pace that our surroundings blur. When we finally slow down, we feel lost. What should we do when we feel this way during a rough spot in life?

Often we feel lost because we have lost our first love (our relationship with Christ is not as intimate as it used to be). Anytime we are lost, or lose something, we must trace our steps backward until we come to the place where things are familiar again, or until we find what we had lost. Another tip when we feel lost is to be willing to listen to directions. In our Christian lives, that happens when we quiet ourselves (*Be still* in Psalm 46:10 means "cease striving") and focus on his Word (from the Bible or from his Spirit).

Everyone knows where Carmen Sandiego is. Some can even answer the question, where's Waldo? But do you know where *you* are? Sometimes we just need to recheck the address!

> Everyone knows where Carmen Sandiego is. Some can even answer the question, where's Waldo? But do you know where *you* are? Sometimes we just need to recheck the address!

Oscar or Felix?

Do you remember *The Odd Couple*? Oscar Madison and Felix Unger shared an apartment. Oscar was messy, unorganized, and laid back. Felix was neat, regimented, and probably would be diagnosed with obsessive-compulsive disorder today. It's amazing these two got along so well. Did you ever wonder how they could be such good friends when they were so different from each other? Perhaps it's because deep down, if you removed all their differences, they both had the same good hearts.

I have certain traits similar to both Oscar and Felix. I'm normally organized and professional when it comes to work and church projects, and I love to dress sharp. But I'm sloppy at home, even when I have the best intentions.

Are you more of a Felix or an Oscar? How does your temperament help or hinder your relationships?

When it comes to reading the Bible, are you more like Oscar or Felix? When Oscars look for wisdom in the Bible, they use the "magic verse" technique. Perhaps you are familiar with this. Oscars flip open the Bible to any page, close their eyes, and point to a verse. This is their verse for the day, and they claim it for any circumstance that comes their way. Oscar types are tempted to procrastinate actually reading the Bible.

Felixes have a systematic, organized technique for reading their Bibles. Perhaps they read through the Bible in a year or use a special Bible study book or some other routine reading schedule. Felix types are more disciplined and read the Bible before they feel a need for biblical direction or advice.

Obviously there are no wrong techniques for Bible reading. God's just glad you want to hear his voice via the Word. When you open the Bible, you are inviting God to speak to you. You learn his heart and grow more like him. The more children spend time with a parent, the more they become *like* that parent. This happens to us when we spend time with our heavenly Father in his Word too.

Are you an Oscar or a Felix? No matter what your personality type, the Bible can direct your life.

Grow with Joy

When I discovered your words, I devoured them. They are my joy and my heart's delight, for I bear your name, O Lord God of Heaven's Armies. (Jeremiah 15:16)

I can think of many food items I've devoured with joy. A hot fudge sundae comes to mind. And Mom's hot rolls. But how often have I actually devoured God's Word? To devour food means to gulp it down like you can't eat fast enough to consume your fill. Do you crave Scripture like you devour food? As we develop a stronger appetite for the Bible, we will also find our joy and delight in it.

> **Do you crave Scripture like you devour food? As we develop a stronger appetite for the Bible, we will also find our joy and delight in it.**

The commandments of the LORD are right, bringing joy to the heart. The commands of the LORD are clear, giving insight for living. (Psalm 19:8)

Most of us will admit it seems impossible at first to find joy in any sort of command. On the surface, rules seem to be demanding and constricting, not freeing and peaceful. Certainly not joyful! Yet Psalm 19:8 tells us God's commands cause joyful hearts. Perhaps it's because his commandments *are right*. This verse goes on to explain that we pick up insight for living because his ways are made clear to us. Joy comes as we realize we don't have to do life alone—his Word guides us as if he's given us our very own driving directions.

Oh, the joys of those who do not follow the advice of the wicked, or stand around with sinners, or join in with mockers. (Psalm 1:1)

One source of joy is knowing we won't allow the wrong crowd to influence us. Not only is it wise to determine not to be impacted by those who don't seek the Lord—it brings joy. Perhaps it comes from knowing God isn't going to let someone else lead us astray as long as we follow him. Can you think of an occasion when you spent time with someone who didn't seek God's ways and it backfired on you?

THE JOY OF DIRECTION AND OBEDIENCE

> *Oh, the joys of those who trust the LORD, who have no confidence in the proud or in those who worship idols.* (Psalm 40:4)

Trusting the Lord brings joy. Trust is relying on God in full confidence that only he is able to do what he says he will do. He has *trustability*. Interestingly, another meaning of *trust* (as a noun) is "expectation." Read Psalm 40:4 with "put their expectations in" substituted for *trust*. We can't put any expectations in the proud or those who have ungodly priorities—if we do, we might experience an absence of joy. (So *that's* where my joy disappears sometimes!)

> *O LORD of Heaven's Armies, what joy for those who trust in you.* (Psalm 84:12)

> *I take joy in doing your will, my God, for your instructions are written on my heart.* (Psalm 40:8)

I find it interesting that people believe God's will is a big mystery—and they embark on a lifelong journey to find it. This passage shows us that God gives us a how-to manual. His instructions are written on our hearts. And when we follow these directions, we experience joy. In fact, the verse says we *take joy*, which means we actively choose to enjoy doing God's will.

> *Light shines on the godly, and joy on those whose hearts are right.* (Psalm 97:11)

If I discovered this verse on social media, I'd click *Like*. I love references to *light* and *shine*. Look what believers get when we seek to be right with God. Light and joy shine on us. How do we make sure our hearts are right? By being godly, which means God is our pattern, or template, for our actions and attitudes. Proverbs 13:9 backs up this principle: *The life of the godly is full of light and joy, but the light of the wicked will be snuffed out.*

> *Praise the LORD! How joyful are those who fear the LORD and delight in obeying his commands.* (Psalm 112:1)

> *How joyful are those who fear the LORD—all who follow his ways!* (Psalm 128:1)

How can we delight in obeying someone we fear? We can when that fear (respect and honor) is based on how awesome and powerful God is. Those who realize how mighty God is follow after him and revere him. And all those who do are joyful—full of joy.

THE GRIN GAL'S GUIDE TO JOY

If your instructions hadn't sustained me with joy, I would have died in my misery. (Psalm 119:92)

God often uses hyperbole in his Word—making exaggerations so we get the contrast. In this case, the psalmist states he would die in misery if he wasn't joyfully sustained through God's instructions.

Can we honestly say we'd be so miserable we might as well die if we didn't have God's Word to sustain us? Consider the word *sustain,* which means "to nourish and support." In order for God's Word to nourish us, we need to make it as high a priority as food—and if God's instructions are to support us, we need to seek him first rather than other forms of support.

Whom do you put in front of God on your support team? Can you think of the last time you called someone or e-mailed a friend rather than praying to God first about a matter?

Maybe a change of priorities will also cause a change in our joy quotient!

As pressure and stress bear down on me, I find joy in your commands. (Psalm 119:143)

Who doesn't have pressure and stress? It certainly does feel like it's bearing down on us, right? But even during stressful times, we can find joy when we seek direction and discernment through God's commands. Often the words *commands, instructions,* and *law* are interchangeable and mean *God's Word*—what we now have as the Bible.

> *Dear brothers and sisters, I close my letter with these last words: Be joyful. Grow to maturity. Encourage each other. Live in harmony and peace. Then the God of love and peace will be with you.* (2 Corinthians 13:11)

Paul gives us some steps to growth. Look at the first step: *Be joyful.* If we try to mature as Christians without joy on board, we are taking the wrong ship to get to our destination. Other passengers on our trip to spiritual maturity include encouraging one another, living in harmony and peace, and experiencing God's abiding presence. Which one of these is the most difficult for you to incorporate fully into your everyday life?

Go with Joy

Why is the simple instruction to be joyful so difficult to manage? For some reason, it's easier for our minds to be drawn to the negative rather than the positive. If you've ever thought any of these thoughts, you know what I mean:

- I wonder what she meant by that statement?
- Easy for her to say—she doesn't have my circumstances.
- Why should I forgive them? They haven't even shown any remorse!
- How will I pay for groceries this week?
- Why did she get that job promotion and not me?
- I'm such a dweeb—why can't I get anything right?

It's human nature to focus on all the things we think God isn't doing in our lives rather than counting our blessings. We'd never admit to blaming God, but that's what we're doing. We want to trade our lives in for something more in line with our expectations, and when we get what we dream of, *then* we will be joyful.

Wrong! Joy can come right now—it doesn't have to wait until morning. It can reside in our hearts even when they are breaking. When we operate out of a mindset of joy, we can change our perspective on our lives, and sometimes that in turn changes our lives! Even when life remains unbearable despite our joy, we at least have contented peacefulness. We can't work up joy, but we can abide in the Christ of joy and allow his perspective to flow through us.

> Joy can come right now—it doesn't have to wait until morning. It can reside in our hearts even when they are breaking.

Action Steps to Joy

Need more joy? Follow these steps from God's Word.

1. **Learn to replace other emotions with joy.** Is there ever a time when joyfulness is not the appropriate mind-set? *Always be joyful* (1 Thessalonians 5:16).

2. **Evaluate if there's any area of disobedience in your life.** Obedience leads to joy; rebellion leads to running. *When people do not accept divine guidance, they run wild. But whoever obeys the law is joyful* (Proverbs 29:18).

3. **Pray a *trust* prayer today—letting go of anything you've been hanging on to.** What causes you to stay in your comfort zone rather than on trusting ground? *Those who listen to instruction will prosper; those who trust the LORD will be joyful* (Proverbs 16:20).

4. **Determine God's ways for your situation and use that realization as a pattern for your own choices.** It really takes just two simple steps: listen to godly wisdom and follow it. *And so, my children, listen to me, for all who follow my ways are joyful* (Proverbs 8:32).

5. **Perform an integrity checkup.** Is there any slipup or choice in your life that reflects poor character? Make it right and you'll discover renewed joy. *Joyful are people of integrity, who follow the instructions of the LORD* (Psalm 119:1).

6. **Seek God with every part of your being.** Are you holding anything back? That choice to restrict God from one part of your life also restricts joy from flowing through you. *Joyful are those who obey his laws and search for him with all their hearts* (Psalm 119:2).

Have you experienced a time when God provided joy through his Word? How did God make it real to you?

Are there any instructions in God's Word that cause you to bristle or resist? Do you have a tendency to ignore it, explain it away, or rebel? Or do you yield—minus the joy? Is there a way to embrace the instruction in a more positive way?

What's one thing you are seeking God's direction or discernment on right now? Explain. How will receiving the answer be a source of joy for you?

Give with Joy

Songs and bumper stickers often misrepresent the Christian life and mislead believers into thinking they will be happy all the time. Happiness is merely a feeling associated with circumstances. It is difficult for any human being to experience happiness 24/7 when God also created other emotions. Even Jesus wept.

Perhaps a country and western song would be more appropriate for our journey: "I Never Promised You a Rose Garden." God didn't tell us life would be hunky-dory after we follow him. He only assures us that he will be with us whether we are in a valley or on a mountaintop, in the storm or viewing the rainbow.

Not a week goes by without someone I care about receiving bad news. And I seem to accumulate trials like valuable collectibles. Bad news tells me trouble abounds. Some people are mocked by family members. Others have heard bad news from medical tests. Business competitors undermine each other. Grandparents end up caring for their grandchildren because the parents are absent or negligent. Church members spread hurtful gossip.

So how do we cope?

First, we pray. We ask God to help us be willing to let go of our problems and let him handle them. We seek his wisdom and his solace. Then we recruit prayer support and encouragement from others. We find those who will empathize and let us lean on them, but we also give others permission to hold us accountable if we need a perspective adjustment.

We also read God's Word for advice and allow Scripture to mold our attitudes and actions. The Bible is as relevant today as when it was inspired.

Finally, we realize our expectations will not fully be met while we are living in this imperfect world. We contribute to this flawed life with our own faults. To overcome these struggles, we learn a better way of dealing with trials. We give others the benefit of the doubt. We recognize that bad things happen to good people. We become proactive and take responsibility for our own lives—to be lived out in a Christ-honoring fashion. We cope. Coping becomes surviving. Surviving leads to thriving. Thriving in the midst of bad news is the miracle—not the rose garden but living out loud despite the thorns. In doing this, we learn how joy can flourish even in the midst of negatives. And when this joy blooms, it is best shared with others.

> Having a foundation built on God's Word is often the absent puzzle piece when joy's gone missing.

Serve It Forward in the Joy of God's Word

Spotlighting God's Word is a great way to help others find a sense of direction in today's scavenger-hunt world. Joy is a happiness that lasts even when good circumstances don't. Are there as many joyful individuals today as there were in years gone by? It certainly seems more people are missing that peaceful inner glow. In this chapter we've learned that having a foundation built on God's Word is often the absent puzzle piece when joy's gone missing.

Some individuals are receptive to us sharing Bible verses with them. Most prefer we share in a spirit of coming alongside rather than as a preacher or expert. No one wants to feel like a project—as if we're trying to *fix* them. (I withdraw when I feel like someone's trying to fix *me*!) So, while God's Word is powerful, it is sometimes best administered in small doses. Sort of like that concentrated detergent I just purchased. If I use too much, the garment isn't merely clean, it's worn out. We don't want to wear out the ones with whom we're sharing Scripture!

Other individuals will respond to an even lighter touch—observing us as we live out the Word more than speaking it directly to them. I think that's why the Bible says we are to be light and salt (Matthew 5:13-16). To some, we are light—reflecting God in our actions and attitudes. And to others we are salt—a medicinal astringent, able to add both flavor and healing. We all need to hear God's Word (how can we change unless we hear?). But it takes discernment and discretion to know how and when to share. Ask God to show you the best way to serve it forward when it comes to spreading the joy of God's Word to others.

Your Grin-with-Joy Challenge

You are so stressed; one trial after another is hitting you right now. You can't understand why this is all happening, so you read your Bible. You know not all trials are caused by rebellion against God, but sometimes they can be indicators that something's amiss regarding your relationship with him. As you read and pray, the Holy Spirit nudges you to think about obedience. There's something you've been holding back when it comes to honoring God. You know it's wrong, but you just can't help it. Or can you? What can you do to deal with this specific choice so you experience the joy of obedience?

Chapter Two

THE WORKS OF *Joy*

Do all the good you can, by all the means you can, in all the ways you can, in all the places you can, at all the times you can, to all the people you can, as long as ever you can. —JOHN WESLEY

God's Word and God's Spirit work in us—we are all works in progress. We in turn produce fruit pleasing to him. Good works are not necessary for salvation, but they are evidence of a life dedicated to Christ. When we operate from hearts of service, we experience joyful enthusiasm and a spirit of gratitude.

Grin with Joy

After eating the best homegrown cantaloupe I'd ever savored, I vowed never to eat another store-bought melon again. A fruity, ripe scent escaped from where the melon had been cut off the vine. Even before I sliced it open, I knew it was going to be delicious—and it did not disappoint! The vibrant fruit flesh oozed juicy flavor. A moist sac encased the seeds in the middle of the fruit. The farmer had separated the fruit from the vine at the best stage of maturity.

This got me to thinking about our Christianity. Do we produce a sweet, savory scent to our heavenly Gardener? Do we pursue the goals we were designed to achieve? Do we follow the "*Heavenly Farmer's Almanac*" (Scripture) to schedule our planting and reaping?

The most important element in being the fruit we were created to be is being firmly attached to the vine. Jesus Christ is the vine—our sustenance. He attaches us to our heavenly Father. Everything that is good and fertile comes when we realize our position in Christ. Only when the time comes for us to be cut from the vine, at our death and graduation to heaven, will our life stories be realized. Until then we have time to grow in him. Even if some get a dry start, our heavenly Gardener will water and fertilize, and tenderly care for each fruit until the day of the harvest.

> When we operate from hearts of service, we experience joyful enthusiasm and a spirit of gratitude.

When we realize we aren't the be all and end all of life within ourselves, and that Jesus, the vine, is our only source of new life and peace, we will be well on our way to producing flavorful fruit.

Abide in me, and I in you. As the branch cannot bear fruit by itself, unless it abides in the vine, neither can you, unless you abide in me. I am the vine; you are the branches. Whoever abides in me and I in him, he it is that bears much fruit, for apart from me you can do nothing. (John 15:4–5 ESV)

Blackberry Patch

One of the hidden benefits of buying our Kentucky home was discovering we owned the woods behind our fenced backyard. My husband cleared out the brush to create various paths. One thing he didn't weed out was the wild blackberry brambles. During the entire process, we eagerly watched the blackberries mature and ripen. First we saw the blossoms, then the fruit appeared, and finally the mature fruit was ready to be picked.

I learned something as I observed the berries' maturation process—blackberries don't all mature at the same rate. Some berries ripened slower than others. Some of the fruit were smaller than others. Worst of all, some fruit didn't ripen at all, but died on the vine. They never matured into plump, juicy, flavorful berries.

We evaluated all the variables and came to some conclusions. The berries in the sun ripened quicker and produced better fruit. The berries choked by other weeds and plants dried up rather than ripened. And berries in the shade eventually ripened with smaller fruit, as long as there was the right amount of rain.

We experience Christian growth similar to these berries. We mature based on circumstances being right. We need to be in the *Son* to mature into the best fruit, as designed by the Creator. Even in partial darkness (focus on self), with some *Son* the fruit will grow, but at a slower rate and with an inferior finished product. Sadly, some Christians allow the cares of life to choke out their spiritual growth, much like the weeds overcame some of our wild berries by wrapping around the brambles—cutting the berries off from nourishment.

I want to produce ripe, juicy fruit. Not for reasons of pride but because I want my Creator to be well pleased. By allowing the Son to shine fully into my life and ignoring my shady self-desire and the choking cares of the world, I will be able to present my mature fruit to the Harvester with great joy.

The Tin Box

I received a tin box stuffed with recipe cards from the World War II era—recipes formulated with one hundred hungry Marines in mind. With limited ingredients on hand, the military kitchen still came up with a large assortment of recipes. Some of these recipes will work great for church events, as long as I don't serve them chipped beef with gravy on toast!

Like these limited-ingredients recipes, there are just a few ingredients required to assemble a godly person. The most important ingredient (the meat) is for the individual to have a personal relationship with Jesus Christ. Not just a belief or a profession, but a familiarity that can only come by spending time with another person in an intimate way. If you can talk to God as easily as you talk to your spouse, your parent, your child, or your best friend, then you experience what I mean by *intimacy*. If you sense God's presence in your daily journey and are conscious of his direction for your life, then you are on intimate terms with your heavenly Father!

When your relationship with God fills the spot designed for the primary ingredient, everything else needed for the recipe of growing godly is provided. (They can be found in God's pantry.) You will exhibit the fruit of the Spirit. Such joy bubbles over, and others *want* what you have! They will know you are Christ centered because of your unconditional love.

What I have discovered, however, is that even though there are few ingredients to the Christian life, there are many manifestations. Just as the Marines were able to make many different dishes from the same few ingredients, God allows us, the church, to be diverse. We sometimes expect every Christian to exhibit the same features, and we might even doubt the sincerity of believers who aren't similar to us. Yet God has made us all different. Rather than asking if others are like us, the important question to ask is, are they like Christ? That is all that really matters!

Let us all pursue those few ingredients that make up real Christlikeness. And let us allow others to be who God wants them to be in Christ. Be all you can be? Nah . . . that's the Army!

Grow with Joy

What a joy it is to recognize the strengths God has placed inside each of us—equipping us not only to expand his kingdom, but also to enjoy the life of serving him.

> **What a joy it is to recognize the strengths God has placed inside each of us—equipping us not only to expand his kingdom, but also to enjoy the life of serving him.**

I know, my God, that you examine our hearts and rejoice when you find integrity there. You know I have done all this with good motives, and I have watched your people offer their gifts willingly and joyously. (1 Chronicles 29:17)

Part of having integrity and good motives is being willing to offer up our giftedness to be used by God without expecting anything in return. When you examine your heart, what gives you cause to rejoice?

Oh, the joys of those who are kind to the poor! The LORD rescues them when they are in trouble. (Psalm 41:1)

One way we find joy in serving God is to be alert to the needs of those around us and to act in kindness and compassion toward them. The Lord is the one overseeing the rescue mission, but sometimes he chooses to use us if we are tuned in to his lead. Is your radar programmed to sense God's nudge and to see the needs of others? How can you fine-tune that sixth sense?

There is joy for those who deal justly with others and always do what is right. (Psalm 106:3)

Those who do not walk in the ways of the Lord or deal with others according to what is right miss out on joy. If you notice your joy being zapped, evaluate if your actions and attitudes are in the right place. Often when these are out of line, joy disappears. Even worse, bitterness creeps in to try to fill the space joy vacates. But if you make the right adjustments, joy returns. Are there any adjustments you need to make to realign with God's principles or how he wants you to treat others?

Knowing this, I am convinced that I will remain alive so I can continue to help all of you grow and experience the joy of your faith. (Philippians 1:25)

Some Christians are missing out on the joy of their faith. They add God to their lives as more of a tradition or ritual or even a good-luck charm—but not an expression of joyful living. The apostle Paul was determined to live long enough to help other believers grow in their experience of joy-filled faith. Today our mission is a similar two-fold focus. First we are to grow during our joyous faith journey, and we also are to stir up that same joy in others as they grow in their faith. Can you think of someone God placed in your life so you would spur on their joy?

But I will rejoice even if I lose my life, pouring it out like a liquid offering to God, just like your faithful service is an offering to God. And I want all of you to share that joy. Yes, you should rejoice, and I will share your joy. (Philippians 2:17–18)

We share joy when we offer our lives for God's use. We experience personal joy, yes. But it's even more than that. We feel a unique heart connection with others who live out their faith in a similar joyful manner and mindset. Why is it we can meet another Christ follower and have an instant bond? It's because God knits us together at the heart when our hearts share a similar joy in him. Unfortunately, our human nature tends to snuff out the joy and replace it with jealousy, insecurity, pride, or ego. We are tempted to compare ourselves to others rather than rejoice with them. What one issue or specific person does God want you to deal with right now so that you are freed from whatever is holding you back? This will help you wholeheartedly rejoicing with others.

> **Why is it we can meet another Christ follower and have an instant bond? It's because God knits us together at the heart when our hearts share a similar joy in him.**

So two good things will result from this ministry of giving—the needs of the believers in Jerusalem will be met, and they will joyfully express their thanks to God. (2 Corinthians 9:12)

The Corinthians had provided funds for the believers in Jerusalem, and Paul noted two ways giving was beneficial: it provided for the needs of the recipients and created joy as they expressed thanksgiving to God. I can imagine the givers also experienced joy. It's rewarding to use what God has entrusted to us to further his work in the lives of others. The gift receivers are transformed by the joy of having their needs met, and we experience the transformation of generous hearts.

Go with Joy

Snow White sang "Whistle While You Work" while she and the seven dwarfs tidied up the cottage. And the dwarfs sang "Heigh-Ho" on their way to work the mines. Singing inspired extra bounce in their steps, but surely their joyous approach to work is merely fantasy. Or is it?

Inexpressible Joy

When I hunt for life-application points in a Bible passage, sometimes I use this exercise: I highlight all the verb phrases and focus on these as action steps, as if they are assignments from God. Look at the following verses from 1 Peter and see what you discover when you recognize all the verb phrases. Does it give you a road map for finding joy in living the Christian life? Fill in the bullet list of these action steps.

> *So be truly glad. There is wonderful joy ahead, even though you have to endure many trials for a little while. These trials will show that your faith is genuine. It is being tested as fire tests and purifies gold—though your faith is far more precious than mere gold. So when your faith remains strong through many trials, it will bring you much praise and glory and honor on the day when Jesus Christ is revealed to the whole world. You love him even though you have never seen him. Though you do not see him now, you trust him; and you rejoice with a glorious, inexpressible joy. The reward for trusting him will be the salvation of your souls.* (1 Peter 1:6–9)

- Be (what)?
- Endure (what)?
- Remain (what)?
- Bring (what)?
- Love (who)?
- Trust (who)?
- Rejoice!

Action Steps to Joy

Take these steps based on the Bible to move toward joy.

1. **Offer God your first fruits.** *Honor the Lord with your wealth and with the firstfruits of all your produce* (Proverbs 3:9 ESV).

2. **Display joy as a fruit of the Spirit.** *But the fruit of the Spirit is love, joy, peace, patience, kindness, goodness, faithfulness, gentleness, self-control; against such things there is no law* (Galatians 5:22–23 ESV).

3. **Start with obedience and the feelings will follow.** *Commit your works to the LORD, and your thoughts will be established* (Proverbs 16:3 NKJV).

4. **Surrender any cause for bitterness.** *Let all bitterness and wrath and anger and clamor and slander be put away from you, along with all malice* (Ephesians 4:31 ESV).

5. **Be alert for opportunities to show compassion.** *But the wisdom from above is first pure [undefiled]; then peace-loving, [courteous, considerate], gentle, reasonable [and willing to listen], full of compassion and good fruits. It is unwavering, without [self-righteous] hypocrisy [and self-seeking guile]* (James 3:17 AMP).

6. **Practice rejoicing with others, even on your bad days.** *Rejoice with those who rejoice, weep with those who weep* (Romans 12:15 ESV).

What is your number one joy zapper? How can you counteract the zapper when it pops into your life and tries to sabotage you?

> No more joy zappers. When someone tries to push your buttons, remind yourself *they* aren't God. Other people don't get to be the boss of your joy!

No more joy zappers. When someone tries to push your buttons, remind yourself *they* aren't God. Other people don't get to be the boss of your joy!

Other than when you are spreading the gospel message, how might people recognize Christ reflected in you and want to know about the hope that lives in you? How do you prioritize your pursuit of joy, since others are less likely to ask you about your hope when joy is absent? What about when you don't feel like pursuing joy?

Can you think of people who have contagious joy? What are their secrets? (If you aren't sure, ask them, and also thank them for spreading joyfulness.)

Is it possible to experience joy in the midst of suffering and trials? Obviously, circumstances cannot be the source for such joy—so what is?

Give with Joy

A senior citizen ministry in New Mexico is called Saints Alive. What a fun play on the expression "Sakes alive!" When we hear *saint*, we often think of those who have passed on or who are members of the "Gray Hair Club." (Although one little girl named Rosa asked the youth pastor if you had to be thirteen to be a member of the Saints Alive group. We just had to chuckle! The innocence of youth.)

On November 1 we celebrate All Saints Day, which is commemorated by different churches in different ways. Some ignore it altogether because they have seen churches distort the definition of *saint*. But in the Bible, every mention of saints refers to all Christians. Because of church tradition and yes, even because of Hollywood, we have changed the connotation of *saint* to mean a particularly righteous and holy person or someone who was officially granted "sainthood" years after death because of their good works, including miracles they are believed to have performed.

The Bible definition of *saint* includes all men, women, boys, and girls who have accepted and received the finished work of Christ as their connection to God. God sees us as saints because we are clothed in Christ's righteousness rather than our own.

I'm glad that my good works aren't weighed against my bad works to determine my entrance into heaven, but we must admit that when we think of saints, those who lived lives that honored God come to our minds. We look up to certain Christians because of their joy-filled faith through good times and bad. Let's show respect to those who have gone before us and left us that legacy.

> The world may never know what we have done for the kingdom of God, but the one who matters most knows!

As we determine to follow in their footsteps by serving God in our ordinary lives, may others recognize and aspire to take pleasure in the same joy we have.

It's a beautiful process. We're inspired by the saints. We live out the same faith and experience joy. Others recognize that joy and embrace the faith walk. And so it continues. The world may never know what we have done for the kingdom of God, but the one who matters most knows!

Too Close to Call

When politics are in high gear, the expression "too close to call" is mentioned regarding certain voting results. There are other situations in life when it is "too close to call." For example, when a person's life ends, and his friends and family not only mourn the loss of life but wonder where he is spending eternity. The reason? His life had no clear-cut Christian witness or fruit. Only God knows the outcome of a person's soul and whether or not they made a decision to receive and follow Christ. Family and friends cling to any possible hope that their loved one is in heaven based on what they have seen in that person's life. Sometimes that verdict is just "too close to call."

For by grace you have been saved through faith. And this is not your own doing; it is the gift of God (Ephesians 2:8 ESV). This tells me that there is nothing we can do to earn our way into heaven. It is a result of faith.

The book of James tells us what lives look like when they live out this faith. James describes the fruit of good works. These works are not performed to earn salvation but rather *because* of salvation. Good acts and attitudes come from a love for the Savior, not from fear or obligation.

I am challenged to live a life worthy of my upward calling. I would never want anyone to have to wonder where I'm spending eternity after I die. Joy radiating from my life is one way others recognize my faith. It is evidence of God being in a preeminent position in my life. Joy can't be worked up in my humanness—it can only be experienced in its purest form when it's a result of God being in first place.

Will others recognize your faith position because of your joy? Or will it be too close to call? Explain.

Serve It Forward in the Joy of Good Works

It's always fun to watch new band students begin toting their instruments home from school. They are instructed to practice. Some students give up before they learn all the basics because practice is such hard work. Parents begin to wonder if it's worth it, because their little Johnny isn't Kenny G in one week's time.

But quitting isn't the answer. Practice is.

As Christians, what are we busy practicing? What image do we portray to others? Do they know we are Christians by our actions and attitudes? We don't *become* Christians by doing good works, but we practice good works *because* of our love for the Savior if we are Christians.

> Being joyful takes practice.

Being joyful takes practice. We have to undo our bad attitudes. We might even have to let go of some religious beliefs that aren't taken from biblical principles.

Like beginner band students, sometimes we make mistakes as we learn how to reflect Christ. But hopefully others will not question our Christianity as long as they see our sincere desire to please God. When we go to a beginner band concert we chuckle at the squeaky woodwinds, the blatting horns, or the off-beat drums. But we don't question whether the performers are band students, because they are sincerely trying. They just have a few more lessons to learn and a lot more practicing to do. Christians also make mistakes along the way. Don't give up trying. Joy takes practice. And practice makes permanent. Just ask Kenny G!

Your Grin-with-Joy Challenge

You've been asked to serve on the team for a new service project at church, but you aren't sure if you should accept. You already have a busy schedule and don't really need to add another obligation. But the service project excites you, and you do have skills that would work well with the rest of the team. And though your current schedule is busy, you haven't been very joy filled lately. Maybe this new project would help you experience more joy as you work alongside others toward a common goal. You're not certain, but it seems as if God might be the one opening the door to this opportunity. Still, how will you manage adding it to your already stressful workload? What do you do?

Chapter Three

THE *Joy* OF THE GOSPEL

Joy is the serious business of heaven. —C. S. Lewis

When Christ began his work on earth, it brought God the Father great joy. Pleasing the Father brought Jesus Christ joy. And the gospel delivers joy to each believer who receives the gift of the good news.

Grin with Joy

The phone rang, and someone with a thick Mexican accent said, "Do you know who this is?"

"You'll have to give me a clue," Russ said. We have many friends whose mother tongue is Spanish. The caller would have to be more specific.

"This is Ramon. Remember me?"

Of course we remembered Ramon and his wife, Maria! Almost twenty years earlier, we frequented Elena's Mexican Restaurant in Beaumont, Texas, when Russ ministered in a nearby town. Maria served as waitress there. She watched us pray at every meal. She came up to us one day and asked us to pray for her baby—he was going to have surgery.

We prayed right then. Her heart was touched by our concern. We asked if she'd like us to visit her home and pray with the family, which thrilled her even more. When we arrived at Maria's home, her *baby* was a teenager! We prayed with Paco and reassured him we were there for him and his family. We didn't stay strangers for long.

We had an instant connection with this family. Even with the language barrier, we made do. When Paco had surgery in Galveston, we were there all day and helped to translate the news from the doctors and nurses (if you call charades and gestures "translating"!).

Maria invited me back to her home because she had many questions about God. I purchased an English-Spanish parallel Bible and encouraged Maria to read the verses in Spanish. She learned that God loved her so much he sent his Son Jesus to die for her sins and for the sins of the world. She read how she could accept that gift through prayer, turning away from her own way and placing her faith in Jesus. She wanted the same joy she saw in me—a peace of mind that would carry her through the tough times and make her feel like soaring during the good times.

> She wanted the same joy she saw in me—a peace of mind that would carry her through the tough times and make her feel like soaring during the good times.

After reading more Bible verses, she asked if she could pray and start her own relationship with God. I welcomed her to pray in Spanish, and we bowed our heads. As she received Jesus into her life, I *cried*. Such a precious heart prayer—I will never forget it (and so thankful I knew enough Spanish to understand it.) She closed with "Gracias, Señor" and we embraced.

Early in our friendship, Ramon invited us to experience menudo for the first time. Not the singing group—tripe stew. Ramon made two versions, one with hominy and one without. I chose the version with hominy; I figured it would have a better feel and taste. Russ chose without. He struggled to swallow the thick chunks of meat rejected by our familiar butchers. Not just tripe, but also some sort of animal joints—maybe pigs feet and chicken feet? I seasoned my bowl with hot peppers and made it through the concoction. Russ's delicate palate refused to let him swallow without gagging. I added a pile of sliced jalapeno to his bowl, acting like he needed to try it with the extra heat. I intended to sabotage the stew so he could declare it too hot to eat. It worked! Ramon offered to get Russ a new bowl of menudo, and Russ declined, saying he was full.

About that time, Maria came home from work with a McDonald's bag in her hand. "Pastor, you eat menudo? *I* no eat menudo!" That was the day we realized we didn't have to fake our way through anything we found unappetizing to befriend this family. Russ could have ordered a hamburger along with Maria. No matter, it was a "happy meal" anyway!

Maria and I rehearsed a song to sing in church together. Her part in Spanish, my part in English, then together—joyful voices lifted in praise to the One who knit our hearts together. Ramon was so loyal to the church and such a hard worker. When we had workdays for people to come help on projects around the church, Ramon was always the last one working. In fact, we had to ask him to leave—so *we* could go home and crash!

I learned about life and death from this family's cultures and traditions. Several loved ones died horrible deaths—some of them young people. Heart-wrenching moans and cries escaped from those left behind as they held twenty-four-hour vigil over the bodies before they were laid to rest. Rubbing alcohol sat at the ready on nearby tables to revive any mourners feeling faint. Deep grief like I've never seen. These people understood the seriousness of life and death. Funerals were such a stark contrast to the parties held for events like weddings and quinceañera celebrations.

Maria and Ramon made us feel a part of their lives, and they were a part of ours. But after we left that ministry twenty years ago, we had lost track of them. Maria couldn't sleep the night after our call—she was so excited to be back in touch with us. This is the joy of the gospel!

And it all started with a hurting mother requesting prayer for her hurting *baby*.

Grow with Joy

Children find great joy in celebrating Christmas and Easter, but it's the gospel message in those two events that provides the bookends for why we can even experience true joy.

> **Children find great joy in celebrating Christmas and Easter, but it's the gospel message in those two events that provides the bookends for why we can even experience true joy.**

I love how the Bible documents the joy unborn John had when his mother, Elizabeth, greeted cousin Mary, bearing the Christ child.

> *I heard your greeting, the baby in my womb jumped for joy.* (Luke 1:44)

Elizabeth, above the age spectrum for giving birth, and Mary, at the starting point of childbearing age. Being in the proximity of Jesus, John jumped for joy. How might we have that same sense of glee when we experience the nearness of Christ in our lives?

> *We do this by keeping our eyes on Jesus, the champion who initiates and perfects our faith. Because of the joy awaiting him, he endured the cross, disregarding its shame. Now he is seated in the place of honor beside God's throne.* (Hebrews 12:2)

It's interesting to view the gospel story from Jesus' point of view. Look at how he is described in this passage and how vital these various locations and positions are to us as the recipient of his important work.

- **Description**. *Champion.*
- **Task**. *Initiates and perfects our faith.* He pursues us first, and when we respond to his presence, he is there to help us mature in the faith. His job isn't over after our first encounter with him.
- **Motivation**. *The joy awaiting him.* I've never seen it described this way before. Do you think it might be describing the joy at returning to heaven, having pleased the Father?
- **Challenges**. *Endured the cross, disregarding its shame.* Think of the ridicule of being publicly put to death in the most painful, shameful and personal manner known to man at that time.
- **Reward**. *Seated in the place of honor beside God's throne.* Other Bible versions say "at the right hand of the Father." It is a place of honor—as it should be!

> *The Holy Spirit, in bodily form, descended on him like a dove. And a voice from heaven said, You are my dearly loved Son, and you bring me great joy.* (Luke 3:22)

Looking at the gospel from the Father's perspective is also exciting! At the beginning of his public ministry, Jesus gave us a pattern for Christian obedience by being baptized. At this event, the heavenly Father announced—louder than an emcee with a PA system turned way up, so there was no doubt in the minds of the witnesses that day—how he feels about his Son. Second Peter 1:17 mentions this same event and describes the voice as being *from the majestic glory of God*. This must have been the source of contagious joy! God treasured his Son and experienced *great joy* because of Jesus. How does the work and person of Jesus Christ bring *us* great joy?

> *In the same way, there is more joy in heaven over one lost sinner who repents and returns to God than over ninety-nine others who are righteous and haven't strayed away! . . . In the same way, there is joy in the presence of God's angels when even one sinner repents.* (Luke 15:7, 10)

The gospel message is important to heaven because our souls are important to God. Every time a person turns from his sin and receives the gift of salvation through the payment Jesus offered on the cross, the angels in heaven rejoice in celebration.

> *But even as he spoke, a bright cloud overshadowed them, and a voice from the cloud said, "This is my dearly loved Son, who brings me great joy. Listen to him."* (Matthew 17:5)

If you read Matthew 17, you'll discover the account of what is known as the transfiguration. This was when Jesus took Peter, James, and John up a mountain and two men from prior times in the history of Israel showed up—Moses and Elijah. It is speculated that Moses and Elijah were there as respected forefathers of the faith, to show Jesus' disciples their endorsement of Jesus' work. God showed up too, as he made his official declaration of endorsement for Jesus a second time.

> *The women ran quickly from the tomb. They were very frightened but also filled with great joy, and they rushed to give the disciples the angel's message.* (Matthew 28:8)

I like to put myself in the sandals of women in the Bible to imagine what they experienced. Try that exercise with the scenario from this passage. You go to where you've heard Jesus is buried, intending to finish the burial customs, since those had been left incomplete due to the Sabbath restrictions. You expect to see the body of Jesus, wrapped in burial cloths. But you haven't really thought this plan through. The stone will be blocking the entrance, right? As you get to the site, an earthquake, along with an angel who rolls the stone away, surprises you. After you see the guards trembling and you receive instruction from the angel, you realize the grave is empty and you run to deliver the angel's message to the disciples. This verse says the women were *very frightened but also filled with great joy*. Imagine you are there. Why are you frightened? Why are you filled with great joy?

> **I like to put myself in the sandals of women in the Bible to imagine what they experienced.**

> *Still they stood there in disbelief, filled with joy and wonder. Then he asked them, "Do you have anything here to eat?"* (Luke 24:41)

After Jesus resurrected from death but before he ascended into heaven to be with the Father, he had several choice encounters with his disciples. This passage documents the amazement of his followers. Can you imagine the joy of seeing Jesus again after thinking he was gone for good?

How do you think this event gave them the ability to say good-bye to Jesus and embrace whatever was next in their spiritual journeys?

> *As he spoke, he showed them the wounds in his hands and his side. They were filled with joy when they saw the Lord!* (John 20:20)

This is another verse taken from the time after Jesus was raised from the dead but before he went to be with the Father in heaven. As much as the disciples must have grieved to see the wounds caused by the crucifixion, that sadness paled in comparison with the joy they experienced to be with him again. Jesus didn't bring up the wounds to overwhelm these followers, but to offer proof of identity. He was no longer dead! And because he lived, these disciples, and all believers from all the ages, have the same hope of being resurrected. We can have joy in knowing we will one day be face to face with our Lord in heaven if we've accepted his gift of salvation and turned from our selfish ways.

Go with Joy

Pregnancies and births are some of the most joyous occasions known to women. Everything from receiving the news "You're pregnant," to the celebration of the baby shower, and to the actual miracle of birth—it's all a reason for joy. Multiply that joy many times over, and we might come close to understanding the joy accompanying the birth of the Christ child. Others anticipated great things with his arrival. Special messages captured the joy of this special time. Because an entire nation anticipated the Savior, it wasn't merely Mary who celebrated the birth and life of Jesus.

- **Shepherds.** Shepherds taking care of their flocks received the news. *The angel reassured them. "Don't be afraid!" he said. "I bring you good news that will bring great joy to all people"* (Luke 2:10).
- **Simeon.** Elderly Simeon had waited to see Jesus—his life desire fulfilled. *Then Simeon blessed them, and he said to Mary, the baby's mother, "This child is destined to cause many in Israel to fall, but he will be a joy to many others. He has been sent as a sign from God, but many will oppose him"* (Luke 2:34).
- **Zacchaeus.** After Jesus began his public ministry, others rejoiced to see Jesus and experience his message and ministry. Zacchaeus, a corrupt tax collector, desired so much to see Jesus that he climbed into a tree. When Jesus saw Zacchaeus there, he invited himself over for dinner. *Zacchaeus quickly climbed down and took Jesus to his house in great excitement and joy* (Luke 19:6).

The Joy of the Gospel

The word *gospel* essentially means "good news." In the case of the gospel of Christ, the good news is that he left heaven to come to earth and be born in human form, lived a sinless live, and took our place—became our substitute. He paid the price for the sins of all humanity. Every person's imperfection causes him or her to make selfish choices, opposite of what God wants us to do—we rebel against Papa God. When we decide we want to go his way in life rather than our own, we have the opportunity to pray and accept his gift of salvation.

> Jesus wants his followers to know the type of joy that doesn't depend on good events but is based on the best news of all—his gospel.

What are we accepting? We are receiving his gift, confessing that we believe Jesus is God's Son, who became the perfect sacrifice for us. God required a sacrifice of death in payment for sin, in order to reconcile sinners to himself. Jesus willingly gave up his life on a cross but did not stay in the grave when he was buried. Three days later he rose from the dead (the resurrection) and spoke to his closest followers again over a period of forty days before ascending into heaven to sit at his Father's right hand at the throne of glory.

When we turn from our own ways to accept this gift, filled with remorse over our sinfulness, we have the hope of going to this same heaven to be with the Father and the Son. We also have the joy of living the rest of our lives knowing his Spirit dwells in us and directs our everyday lives. We still have freedom to choose whatever way we will go, but as we make him Lord of our lives, we yield our own desires and instead choose to follow his direction and purpose. We gain knowledge of this wisdom as we pray, read and study the Bible, follow the advice of godly mentors, and heed the principles we learn from sermons as well as other Christian materials.

Action Steps to Joy

Need more joy? Follow these steps from God's Word, focusing on the gospel.

1. **Worship.** The act of worship leads to joy. *So they worshiped him and then returned to Jerusalem filled with great joy* (Luke 24:52).

2. **Anticipate the good still to come when we reach heaven.** *Because of our faith, Christ has brought us into this place of undeserved privilege where we now stand, and we confidently and joyfully look forward to sharing God's glory* (Romans 5:2).

3. **Listen to the teachings of Jesus and possess his joy.** Jesus prayed to the Father prior to being arrested and sent to the cross. He desired for his followers to be filled with the same joy he experienced. He told them as much as he could to prepare them to experience joy even though he knew the terrible circumstances about to come. Jesus wants his followers to know the type of joy that doesn't depend on good events but is based on the best news of all—his gospel. One way we can have that same joy is to read all of the many things Jesus told the disciples. *I told them many things while I was with them in this world so they would be filled with my joy* (John 17:13b).

What is the gospel message, in a nutshell?

If you have experienced the joy of the gospel, describe it. If you haven't yet accepted Jesus' gift of salvation, think about the reasons why. What would be one good reason to accept his gift?

What do you think is different about the joy we have here on earth compared to the joy we will have in heaven?

Give with Joy

A young girl attended Vacation Bible School and had an eventful day. During snack time, some food lodged in her airway, and she couldn't breathe. As Angie turned blue, the helpers all looked on, feeling helpless. One teacher rushed her to the office, where I took charge. I quickly reassured Angie that she would be okay, and I performed the Heimlich maneuver. Out popped the offending morsel. Soon Angie's face pinked back up. We hugged, and she returned to her class. After she left, the seriousness of the situation squeezed my heart. I wilted in gratitude that the Lord allowed me to remain calm enough to rescue this sweet child.

The teacher who brought Angie to me apologized for panicking. She had been trained in advanced first aid for her position as a schoolteacher, but in the terrifying moment, she froze. We both praised the Lord for performing a miracle that day. Our joy level bumped up a notch as we celebrated the good news of Angie's safety. But our joy had yet another opportunity to increase.

> She went home that day with a new joy, and the rest of us basked in the joy of the gospel—glad tidings of good news!

Later, during time for prayer, Angie returned to talk to me. She wanted to know more about being a Christian. After she placed her faith in Jesus as Savior, she exclaimed with exuberance, "Mrs. Kathy, you saved me *twice* today!" We reassured her that it was actually Jesus who saved her both times. He healed her, body and soul. She went home that day with a new joy, and the rest of us basked in the joy of the gospel—glad tidings of good news!

Serve It Forward in the Joy of the Gospel

Accept the challenge of spreading the joy of the gospel by telling someone else about the gift of salvation available to them. Don't worry about having the right words. Just share your story—how has Jesus made a difference in your life? Start out with the basics of the gospel—the events we celebrate at Christmas and Easter. Can you think of others who would benefit from some extra joy? Find out if they've placed their trust in Jesus Christ. It's possible they made a decision to follow him some time ago and somehow got off the path. Encourage them to come back to him, and offer to be their friend in the faith so they don't feel like they are alone in their walk with the Lord. If your friend or loved one has never accepted God's gift of new life, offer to pray with them. There's no magic prayer, so it's fine to pray whatever is on your heart, but if you want a pattern to follow, here's a sample:

> Heavenly Father, I thank you for sending your Son Jesus Christ to earth to live a perfect life and die on the cross to pay the price for my sin. I don't measure up to your holiness and have put myself first. Please forgive my sinful choices and attitudes. No longer do I want to do things my way. I yield to you, to your direction, and I accept your gift of grace in the form of salvation today. Thank you for forgiving me and for receiving me as your child. From this day forward, I am eager to grow in my relationship with you and experience your joy. In Jesus' name, amen.

Your Grin-with-Joy Challenge

You have a friend who seems to actually enjoy delivering other people's bad news to you. She must think she wins a prize if she's the first one in the know about a tragic situation. She zaps your joy. But now some of her tendency to gossip has rubbed off on you. You catch yourself spreading bad news, and it's diminishing your joy even more. What do you do?

Chapter Four

THE CELEBRATION OF *Joy*

If you have no joy, there's a leak in your Christianity somewhere. —BILLY SUNDAY

We have reason to celebrate as we receive the blessings bestowed to us from the Father. He has done amazing things—what good news! We place our trust in him and experience joyful gladness. We can be of good cheer when we commemorate his work.

Grin with Joy

For Russ's birthday, I poured an entire bowl of steaming-hot miso soup all over my front at a hip new Japanese restaurant. I had to sit through the remainder of the meal wearing soaked clothing, which covered up the angry red skin underneath. Not to be outdone, I managed to provide an even more outlandish stunt for our twenty-fifth wedding anniversary.

We made plans to celebrate our silver anniversary by indulging in a once-in-a-lifetime dining experience at a fancy-schmancy restaurant boat on the Ohio River. I primped in preparation. Makeup and a dressy pantsuit. I confess . . . Russ helped zip up my pants, not because they were tight but because the top clasp was broken. I gripped the ends of the waistband together while he yanked the zipper up. I was determined to make it work for our special night out. Granny would have called it getting gussied up.

A valet parked our minivan, making Russ regret that we didn't bring our Monte Carlo SS. Silly us, sometimes we forget to even pretend to be classy! We nearly pranced into the restaurant, soaking up all the ambiance and fussy wait staff. Our table was situated on the window side of the restaurant, with a view of the river and the beautiful Cincinnati skyline. We splurged and ordered surf and turf (a petite lobster tail and specialty steak, aged to perfection). Four servers were assigned to our table, to assist our every need.

One thing I need to mention, before we go further: I'm not always the best planner when it comes to thinking through the repercussions of taking my medications at certain times of day. Before the main course, my diuretic kicked in. When I rose from my seat, a uniformed host escorted me to the powder room. All was well until I tried to zip up. The zipper was stuck. I tried every trick, but the zipper would not budge. I thought I needed a different angle, so I took off the slacks and tried again. Nothing. Since I had a tunic-style top, I tried tucking the offending waistband into the elastic of my white granny panties, but that didn't work. I racked my brain and could not think of any MacGyver-type trick to solve the dilemma. I considered my options: stay in the bathroom the rest of the night until Russ retrieved me or go back to my seat, hoisting up my pants with *discreet* hands, and make the best of the situation.

I decided to face the world bravely, and out the door I went. I held my head high, hoping not to draw attention to my awkward walk. I looked like I had a disorder. (Well, a disorder other than the ones I really have!)

Russ guessed right away what happened. I tried to assure him that it would not keep me from having a good time. I enjoyed the company, the view, the service, and the food. It was a fabulous experience, and having a sense of humor helped me make the best of a terrible situation.

> **No possible shame can shadow the joy of celebration.**

I had to make yet another trip to the powder room thanks to that tardy diuretic. This time, I tried to remove a safety pin Russ had used to gather my bra straps closer to the middle. At the time it seemed like such a brilliant idea to keep my straps tucked in under the sleeveless top. I learned a new rule: if it takes two people to get you dressed, it's going to take two people to undo the damage as well. I squirmed every which way to get out of the undergarment in order to retrieve that safety pin. I used brute force, and the explosion of energy broke off the head of the safety pin, releasing just the straight, pointy part for me to use to fix my pants. I poked the pin through the material on each side of the zipper and bent the metal into a makeshift closure. The metal *arrow* went directly into my skin, so not to be jabbed any worse, once again I walked like a duck back to the table.

It could have been one of Alexander's terrible, horrible, no good, very bad days (like the book by Judith Viorst). But I decided to focus on the positive and make the most of my evening. It was one of those times that the joy of Jesus superseded the disasters. In the full scheme of things, it wasn't going to be the end of the world if my pants fell down, but it did matter that I showed my dear husband the appreciation of twenty-five good years.

We walked out arm in arm, wondering if maybe we took my secret with us. Somehow, I'm sure I made a scene. Certainly there were a few snickering spectators, hiding laughter behind napkins—the proper barrier of decency. Whether it's soup-soaked pants or a goofy prevent-pants-falling duck walk, no possible shame can shadow the joy of celebration.

Grow with Joy

While many of the rules in the law of the Old Testament are no longer applicable in this New Testament age of grace, they are included in the Bible not only to teach us the history of our faith, but to share principles appropriate for any believer.

> *For seven days you must celebrate this festival to honor the* Lord *your God at the place he chooses, for it is he who blesses you with bountiful harvests and gives you success in all your work. This festival will be a time of great joy for all.* (Deuteronomy 16:15)

Festivals were a time for great joy; celebrating the blessings God endowed, including the ability for the people to be successful in their work. When was the last time you celebrated the blessings and successes that come from God? (Note: they *all* come from him!)

> *There was great joy in the city, for Jerusalem had not seen a celebration like this one since the days of Solomon, King David's son.* (2 Chronicles 30:26)

It's neat to see the happiness of this city. Good news, celebrations, and joy go together.

> *We were filled with laughter, and we sang for joy. And the other nations said, "What amazing things the LORD has done for them."* (Psalm 126:2)

The more I study laughter in the Bible, the more I see that it can be an act of worship as well as an outburst of joyous celebration. When I observe sad-sack believers who seem to have lost all hope, peace, and joy, I wonder how effective they are in reflecting Christ to others, especially those who don't have a relationship with the Lord yet. But look what happens when others observe a child of God filled with laughter and singing for joy. People take notice and testify that the Lord is doing amazing things. What would happen if we abandoned our discouragement and pity parties and made sure we tapped into the source of true joy in such a way that it was evident to others?

> *Yes, the LORD has done amazing things for us! What joy!* (Psalm 126:3)

One way to increase our joy is to list the amazing things God has done for us. We tend to do the opposite. We are happiest when we're miserable, it seems! We rehearse all the terrible, awful things we've endured rather than reminding ourselves of the blessings. But the more we focus on our trials, the easier bitterness becomes. We end up convincing ourselves, and trying to convince others, that we are suffering martyrs, deserving of all pity. This sinks us into a deeper and deeper pit of despair. According to this verse, what is one way to get out of the pity pit and embrace joy?

THE CELEBRATION OF JOY

A cheerful look brings joy to the heart; good news makes for good health. (Proverbs 15:30)

If you're happy and you know it . . . tell your face! And then look what happens. Our grin face graces someone else with joy. And when we speak good things, we deliver good health. We don't want to "fake it 'til we make it" because we're all about being real, not fake. So try changing up that saying to "Faith it 'til you make it." We could all use a hefty dose of that good medicine.

At the end of the celebration, Solomon sent the people home. They were all joyful and glad because the Lord had been so good to David and to Solomon and to his people Israel. (2 Chronicles 7:10)

Can you recall the joy you experienced as you left a particularly good party? What would it take for you to experience that same abundance of joy on a regular day?

Nehemiah continued, "Go and celebrate with a feast of rich foods and sweet drinks, and share gifts of food with people who have nothing prepared. This is a sacred day before our Lord. Don't be dejected and sad, for the joy of the Lord is your strength!" . . . So the people went away to eat and drink at a festive meal, to share gifts of food, and to celebrate with great joy because they had heard God's words and understood them. . . . Everyone who had returned from captivity lived in . . . shelters during the festival, and they were all filled with great joy! The Israelites had not celebrated like this since the days of Joshua son of Nun. (Nehemiah 8:10, 12, 17)

The book of Nehemiah chronicles the rebuilding of the Jerusalem wall after exile. Nehemiah organized the work and assigned the tasks. A celebration broke out when the repair was complete and the law that had been given by God to Moses was read aloud to everyone. Nehemiah emphasized the vitality of God's Word for everyday life, and God's Word was given a position of importance among God's people once again. The people responded with great joy as they celebrated this high spot in their history. A party with delicious foods and beverages, gifts, and music. They celebrated not only being right with God again, but also an entirely new sense of freedom.

Has there been a church, family, or community celebration that meant a great deal to you? How might you continue the tradition of gathering in a group to celebrate God's goodness?

Many sacrifices were offered on that joyous day, for God had given the people cause for great joy. The women and children also participated in the celebration, and the joy of the people of Jerusalem could be heard far away. (Nehemiah 12:43)

At the dedication of the wall, people offered sacrifices because their joy overflowed. They recognized it was God who had blessed them with this joy. The noise from this celebration could be heard at a far distance. Don't you imagine those who weren't attending the party wondered about the cause of the commotion? Perhaps there are times it's good to leave others guessing what we're up to as we celebrate God's blessing. Maybe they will be drawn to the party first by curiosity but stay because they see our joy and want that same experience.

The only way for us to experience more joy is to practice celebrating in our everyday lives.

Go with Joy

The only way for us to experience more joy is to practice celebrating in our everyday lives. If we wait until we feel joyous, we'll miss out on enjoying today's blessings from the Lord. Think of ways you can practice being more joyful—especially during times when you feel the least amount of joy.

Read the following verse and fill in the blanks below: *The LORD is my strength and shield. I trust him with all my heart. He helps me, and my heart is filled with joy. I burst out in songs of thanksgiving* (Psalm 28:7).

You will be able to celebrate when you:

- Get your _____ from the Lord.
- Make him your _____ (your protector).
- T_____ him with _____ your heart.
- Receive help from _____.
- Experience a heart _____ with joy.
- You will you know you've done all this when you
- Burst out in _____.

When was the last time you felt this way?

Maybe it's time to celebrate his good news again.

Action Steps to Joy

1. **Make it a daily exercise to seek and praise him to move toward joy!** All who seek the Lord not only praise him, they also experience the effervescence of everlasting joy. *The poor will eat and be satisfied. All who seek the LORD will praise him. Their hearts will rejoice with everlasting joy* (Psalm 22:26).

2. **Raise the volume on your celebration. Sometimes joy is loud.** It might mean you raise your voice in excitement, matching the intensity of your heart jumping up and down. Or perhaps you increase the volume as you listen to or play music. Celebrations are rarely

quiet affairs. And joy doesn't have to be so solemn that you don't feel excitement. *So the people of Israel who were present in Jerusalem joyously celebrated the Festival of Unleavened Bread for seven days. Each day the Levites and priests sang to the* Lord, *accompanied by loud instruments* (2 Chronicles 30:21).

3. **Extend your normal time for thanking God during your personal worship.** When was the last time you allowed God some extra time (for prayer, worship, or devotions) because you experienced extreme joy? *The entire assembly then decided to continue the festival another seven days, so they celebrated joyfully for another week* (2 Chronicles 30:23).

We've all heard of parties that got out of hand in a negative way, but can you think of an event where the celebration showcased the joy of the Lord? When people left the party, what was the emotion they took with them?

You can make an ordinary day a celebration by concentrating on the amazing good things the Lord has done for you. Make a list of the big and small blessings you've experienced in the last month.

Some claim to be glass-half-full or glass-half-empty sort of people. We tend to be wired to look at life with either optimism or pessimism. How are you wired? What can you do differently to increase your level of joy? (Note: it's possible to be realistic while also experiencing joy and contentment. Rather than excuse your inability to look at the positive side by saying "That's just the way I'm wired," focus on the principle "I'm a new creature in Christ. I can learn a new way by patterning my life after the life of Christ.")

> You can make an ordinary day a celebration by concentrating on the amazing good things the Lord has done for you.

Give with Joy

How can the celebration of joy be given away? When the elation of the gospel bubbles up inside of you it spills over and becomes contagious.

Serve It Forward in the Joy of Community Celebrations

Have you ever been involved in a church- or faith-based block party? When I consider the potential of spreading the gospel through the act of celebration, my mind thinks of block parties. It doesn't take much to gather a crowd. Interestingly, it takes the same ingredients we discovered in this chapter's *Grow with Joy* section:

- Excitement and enthusiasm
- Food
- Gifts
- Sacrificial spirit
- Music
- Loud celebration
- Spirit of happiness and festivity

When we prepared for our last block party, we planned for plenty of good food. (Hint: cook some of the food outdoors at the beginning of the event so the savory smell will draw people.) We promoted the event in advance by handing out flyers and invitations, posting signs, and placing an ad in the newspaper. We made sure our regular church attendees knew this was an outreach event and encouraged them to invite others outside the church who weren't part of another church family. A stage became the anchor of the event, where our emcee announced different fun functions and musical groups. Happy, uplifting music of all styles played through the loudspeakers. Live music is best, but recorded music is fine if you can't acquire a band or musical group.

> **Dream big and plan even bigger—you never know what God might do.**

Consider the guests you hope to attract. Make sure you have activities they will enjoy (age-appropriate, G-rated fun). It was neat to see our neighbors walk onto our property. Some were shy at first, curious to see what we had to offer. They were attracted by the music and food, but they were drawn in because of the joy and love they saw in us.

You might need an enormous sign or a big eye-catching vehicle with a sign on it at the corner of your lot to draw a crowd. Sometimes the stage and music are enough to attract attention. The big thing is to make sure you have enough of everything to go around. Dream big and plan even bigger—you never know what God might do. If there are leftover prizes or food, you can donate them to a charity or mission the next day.

If you need to do something on a smaller scale, consider using the outdoors of your home. In several of our homes, we've invited our neighbors to an open house right after we moved in and did some renovations. We knew they were curious about these new people on their street. So we asked friends to help us have a wide array of food lined up on tables, with plenty of refreshing beverages to wash it all down. We parked elsewhere and set up chairs under the carport. We gave curious neighbors a house tour and had a friend sing and play guitar music. I did a funny reading. We played games. And mostly, we had fun!

So whether you initiate a gathering at your house or plan a bigger block party, you can spread your joy through celebrating the good news.

The word *hospitality* in Scripture often refers to entertaining strangers—rather than simply having your closest friends over again. Ask God if there's a way you can serve it forward by spreading your joy to people outside your closest circle of friends. You never know what God might do.

One last word to the wise: be sure to get a noise permit if your municipality requires one. Not every neighbor likes to hear your happiness in their airwaves! Be courteous as you select your volume level, but don't be afraid to draw a crowd. It's all about "happy, happy, joy, joy!"

Your Grin-with-Joy Challenge

One of the morning shows on TV recommends the best way to keep a husband happy is never to quit treating him like he's your boyfriend. The advice serves as a lightbulb moment for you. You realize you've lost the joy of celebrating relationship and have entered a rather mundane routine stage in your marriage. What can you do to increase the joy quotient in your marriage?

Chapter Five

THE *Joy* OF CORRECTION AND FORGIVENESS

> The walls we build around us to keep sadness out also keeps out the joy. —Jim Rohn

Because God loves us, he corrects us. There is joy even in his discipline, as we see his hand on our lives. As we accept his forgiveness and extend forgiveness to others, guilt is cleared and joy flourishes. We rejoice as sin is wiped clean and relationships are restored.

Grin with Joy

As a kid I laughed at the hilarious skit on *Laugh-In* called "The Judge." The actors changed with the seasons, but in the final year of the show, Sammy Davis, Jr., made an entrance into court, clad in a black magistrate's robe, singing, "If your lawyer's sleepin', better give him a nudge! Everybody look alive, 'cause here come de judge! Here come de judge!" Today when I watch judges on television, there's little humor, but certainly plenty of drama.

Perhaps I like court TV because the judge gets to say things I'd love to say in order to right the wrongs in this world. They sometimes even go so far as to preach at the offender, when necessary, in hopes of a wake-up call—a reality check. It amazes me, the different types of people who show up on these programs. Do they not have a clue that the judge will chew them to shreds?

I served as a victim's advocate for a local domestic violence shelter. During one of our court cases, we provided photos to the judge, indicating the brutality of the injuries caused by the batterer. We showed not only the abuse he had already done, but also what he was capable of doing. I'd like to think our court systems are always fair, but unfortunately there are times when the innocent are convicted and the guilty go free—in this case the wife beater walked. The victim didn't receive justice; it taught her once again, life isn't always fair. But because of the law of reaping and sowing found in the Bible, we can hold on to peace of mind, knowing that sometime, somewhere, the offender will come face to face with his offenses and will be held accountable for them.

> I'm grateful to know there is one Judge who is fair. And I'm equally grateful for a Redeemer who has paid the price of that sin so the Judge looks at my case and proclaims, "Pardoned!"

I'm grateful to know there is one Judge who is fair. He desires justice. He holds the sinner accountable for sin. And I'm equally grateful for a Redeemer who has paid the price of that sin so the Judge looks at my case and proclaims, "Pardoned!"

What advocate will represent you on Judgment Day? May Jesus be both attorney and reparation in your case. What a day that will be!

Delete and Undo

We discovered a free computer program to retrieve data deleted by mistake. It's almost like the Easy Button a famous office supply chain sells, only it is the *undo* button. This program allowed me to retrieve some precious photos that were deleted by mistake. I thought these photos were gone forever, so you can imagine my joy when they returned to my computer screen, good as new. I'm grateful for that program, but it made me think of other things I wish I could undo.

Oh, if only I could undo some of the silly things I've done in my life! I would take back some words said, react differently to aggravating circumstances, and just plain ol' *do better*. But unfortunately I can't undo what has been said and done. I *can* do better today. And tomorrow. And the next day.

The only one who has the power to erase is our Lord Jesus Christ. It isn't a special computer program that erases our sins so he sees them no more. It is the price he paid on the cross. All we have to do is admit we messed up (like I had to admit when those photos were deleted) and accept the free gift (just like getting that free software program). I'm so glad God is willing to erase my errors.

But you know what? Because of Christ's sacrificial act of love on the cross, I am motivated to want to do better. I don't have to do better to earn the program or to erase the bad stuff, but I want to do better because of this gift.

Just like I want to be more careful with my computer data (even though I know there is a program to undo the error), I want to be careful with my words and my actions. And even though I can't undo what was done in the past, I can attempt to repair the damage by approaching the ones I've let down. If I go to them with a humble attitude of remorse and let them know just how sorry I am, maybe I have a chance for a do over.

I'm so glad God granted me a do over, and even erased what was done in the past, so I can have a blank canvas. I want to use that fresh start responsibly—to glorify him.

Grow with Joy

Children often try to hide when they want to disobey their parents. Normally, I was an obedient child, but there were times my ideas got me into trouble. One time, I wanted to drink a glass of water in my bedroom, but I was too young to carefully hold a glass, so I was restricted to the kitchen. To prove to myself I was grown-up enough not to spill a drop from the glass, I decided I'd drink it in my bedroom anyway. Only one problem: I couldn't reach up to grab a glass from our cabinet. So I crept up the stairs (also not allowed) to knock on the door of our upstairs renter. I asked her in my sweetest little girl voice if I could please have a cup of water. She must have figured I was playing tea party or something, because she graciously gave me a glass of water.

I remember after her door closed I faced all those stairs going down to our home on the first floor. It seemed like a mountain, and I was no mountain goat! Every step I took was deliberate and cautious—I was careful to watch the rim of the glass to make sure I didn't slosh the water. Slowly, and not so sure-footed, I walked down each step. I felt like such a grown-up, to be able to drink water in my bedroom. I don't remember the rest of the story—I guess I took the glass back up to our neighbor. But I do remember that

> When God forgives us, he puts our sins out of sight—as if he'd never seen them. Joy comes from the *relief* of forgiveness. A relationship restored. Forgiveness brings joy!

after I came to my senses, I didn't like the feeling of being sneaky. I wanted to be a good girl. I didn't like disobeying Mommy and Daddy. I hid the evidence. I didn't want them to know.

Psalm 32:1 and Romans 4:7 both tell us, *Oh, what joy for those whose disobedience is forgiven, whose sins are put out of sight.* We can't hide our wrongdoing from God—he sees it all. When God forgives us, he puts our sins out of sight—as if he'd never seen them. Joy comes from the *relief* of forgiveness. A relationship restored. Forgiveness brings joy!

God's Correction Brings Joy

It seems impossible for correction to actually stimulate joy, but when we adjust our attitudes and actions to align with the Bible and receive God's forgiveness, we reap renewed joy.

> *Joyful are those you discipline, Lord, those you teach with your instructions.* (Psalm 94:12)

When you examine God's instructions and implement them, you will find increased joy. How might his to-dos bring discipline and, eventually, joy?

> **Our joy comes from knowing he loves us and is eager to help us have a good spiritual outcome as well as a closer relationship with him.**

Think of personal trainers at the gym. They give instructions and motivate us to be more disciplined. They are hard on us because they want what is best for us. *Discipline* as a verb, in the sense of God disciplining us, can also bring joy. Our joy comes from knowing he loves us and is eager to help us have a good spiritual outcome as well as a closer relationship with him. Correction and discipline in this sense are good things, even though unpleasant at the time.

THE JOY OF CORRECTION AND FORGIVENESS

*For the LORD disciplines those he loves, and he punishes each
one he accepts as his child. (Hebrews 12:6)*

*For the LORD corrects those he loves, just as a father corrects
a child in whom he delights. (Proverbs 3:12)*

God's forgiveness brings joy, but God's correction can also bring joy. Being corrected is never fun, so how is it believers can find joy in being corrected by God? According to these verses, whom does God discipline? Does that factor in to how God's children can find joy when they are corrected by him?

The late coach of the Dallas Cowboys, Tom Landry, said this about correction: "The job of a football coach is to make men do what they don't want to do, in order to achieve what they've always wanted to be." Correction bends us in a new direction so we can end up achieving not only what we want but, more importantly, what God wants in our lives.

Yes, what joy for those whose record the LORD has cleared of sin. (Romans 4:8)

*Therefore, since we have been made right in God's sight by faith, we have peace with
God because of what Jesus Christ our Lord has done for us. (Romans 5:1)*

*Yes, what joy for those whose record the LORD has cleared of guilt,
whose lives are lived in complete honesty! (Psalm 32:2)*

Imagine a ledger with all your sins listed. I don't know about you, but even though I've tried to live a good-girl life, I have messed up enough that the ledger would be quite thick. Hearing God has a way of erasing that record brings joy! How can living in complete honesty with God and others bring about the joy of a clear record?

Go with Joy

After King David committed adultery with Bathsheba and she became pregnant, he arranged for her husband to be killed in war. He schemed a wily cover-up so he wouldn't be caught. The prophet Nathan came to him, and after giving David several opportunities to come clean, said, "You're the man, David!" David came face to face with his sin and it grieved him, because it grieved God. Read through the following passage—part of a psalm written by David as he approached God with a repentant heart. See how he felt about receiving God's forgiveness.

> [1] *Have mercy on me, O God,*
> *because of your unfailing love.*
> *Because of your great compassion,*
> *blot out the stain of my sins.*
> [2] *Wash me clean from my guilt.*
> *Purify me from my sin.*
> [3] *For I recognize my rebellion;*
> *it haunts me day and night.*
> [4] *Against you, and you alone, have I sinned;*
> *I have done what is evil in your sight.*
> *You will be proved right in what you say,*
> *and your judgment against me is just.*
> [5] *For I was born a sinner—*
> *yes, from the moment my mother conceived me.*

⁶ But you desire honesty from the womb,
teaching me wisdom even there.
⁷ Purify me from my sins, and I will be clean;
wash me, and I will be whiter than snow.
⁸ Oh, give me back my joy again;
you have broken me—
now let me rejoice.
⁹ Don't keep looking at my sins.
Remove the stain of my guilt.
¹⁰ Create in me a clean heart, O God.
Renew a loyal spirit within me.
¹¹ Do not banish me from your presence,
and don't take your Holy Spirit from me.
¹² Restore to me the joy of your salvation,
and make me willing to obey you.
¹³ Then I will teach your ways to rebels,
and they will return to you.
¹⁴ Forgive me for shedding blood, O God who saves;
then I will joyfully sing of your forgiveness.
¹⁵ Unseal my lips, O Lord,
that my mouth may praise you.

(Psalm 51:1–15)

Action Steps to Joy

The previous psalm provides a clear path to joy through forgiveness. Which of these steps do you need to follow today?

1. Ask for God to erase your sin because of his mercy. (vv. 1, 7, 9, 14)
2. Receive God's forgiveness to eradicate your guilt feelings. (v. 2)
3. Admit you rebelled against God by trying to please your own desires rather than seeking his will. (vv. 3–4, 10)
4. Rejoice in his forgiveness and take joy in obeying him. (vv. 8, 12)
5. Draw close to God in fellowship. (v. 11)
6. Teach others these same principles. (v. 13)
7. Praise God. (vv. 14–15)

Think of a time when you forgave someone who "did you wrong." Describe the joy you experienced from being free of the hurt and pain after you forgave them.

Most Christ followers can recall the joy that flooded their hearts and minds when they first became believers. What do you remember of that time? What made it so special?

Have you ever been forgiven by someone else when you messed up and you knew you didn't deserve forgiveness? What did their gift of forgiveness mean to you?

Give with Joy

It's impossible to give away joy while harboring unforgiveness, but forgiveness can be part of how you give joy away.

Serve It Forward in the Joy of Forgiveness

They didn't ask me to forgive them, and they didn't admit they did anything wrong. But I knew I needed to forgive them. The unforgiveness in my heart would turn to bitterness if I didn't let go of the hurt as well as release the ones who hurt me into the hands of God.

Have people ever disrespected you, made you feel like less a person, and told you with their actions that you have less worth than others? Then you know my pain. I tried to make things right with them, but they would not bend from their position of rightness.

> It's impossible to give away joy while harboring unforgiveness, but forgiveness can be part of how you give joy away.

What did I do when they dashed my peacemaking efforts? I took it to Jesus. I asked him to heal my breaking heart and to help me get over my feelings of rejection. I was in a bad place. Hurt. Pain. You've been there. What can you do to soothe the sting?

I asked God to help me love these souls with the love of Jesus. That same love Jesus showed me when I didn't deserve love, I wanted to experience for those who sinned against me. I prayed for them. I put myself in their shoes. I gave them the benefit of the doubt—the benefit of grace. And I spoke, "I forgive you." The words didn't pardon the offense, but they said, "I no longer hold you accountable for that, but rather I release you to God, who will take care of helping you grow from this." And he is helping *me* grow from it as well.

Are there people you need to forgive? Maybe this week you can take the first step in learning to love them again, with the same love Jesus has offered you. It's not easy, but it can be done. And you know what happens when you release the hurt? It frees you up to experience unexplainable peace and joy from the God of all comfort. Exchanging hurt for healing and bitterness for blessing—what a trade!

Your Grin-with-Joy Challenge

The women's ministry director at your group discusses the joy of Christ, and you feel like you are missing out on a special blessing. The leader provides a checklist of issues that keep believers from experiencing joy. One of the entries says a lack of forgiveness leads to bitterness, not joy. You face the fact that you have never forgiven that person who wronged you. Your joy has fallen flat ever since. How can you rectify the problem?

Chapter Six

THE *Joy* OF REFUGE AND RENEWAL

> Joy is peace dancing. Peace is joy at rest.
> —Frederick Brotherton Meyer

God provides us with the safety of his refuge. He ransoms us with the sacrifice of his Son. And he renews us to live fully in him. We rejoice as we savor his goodness. Our joy is elevated to new heights as we experience his unfailing love.

Grin with Joy

Tina stood talking with some of the other ladies after church. I watched her daughter Allison cling to her leg. I love these little leg huggers. They sneak up to your side and wrap their tiny arms around your leg since they're too short to receive a full embrace. Tina wore a flouncy broom skirt, and before long, Allison nearly disappeared in the folds of the skirt. Lost in the refuge of her mother's love—safe and secure.

Probably one of the most touching photo stories I've ever witnessed documented the love of a mother hen who drew all her baby chicks underneath her feathers to protect them from a raging fire. Later, rescuers discovered the hen's charred carcass and gave it little thought. Loss of epic proportions filled the area, and rescue noises almost drowned out the sound of tiny chicks, very much alive, chirping under their mother's wings. Perhaps those peeping sounds indicated part panic and part joy of being saved from the horrific smoke and flames. The chicks knew the joy of refuge, made more valuable because it cost their mother's life.

Psalm 91:4 describes how God provides us a similar refuge: *He will cover you with his feathers. He will shelter you with his wings. His faithful promises are your armor and protection.*

Gated Community

The gates went up—temporary walls providing safety and barriers. This was not a great divide between two nations. We installed baby gates to block off the guest bedroom and the family room, two areas where our elderly calico, Libby, hung out. Why? Because our three-month-old Boston terrier had learned to permeate the smaller barriers we previously used. So we brought out the big guns. Boundaries made of wood.

> **May the Father of protection place a wall around you to keep you safe and strengthen you to withstand whatever might tempt or harm you. Take joy in the refuge of boundaries.**

It was interesting to watch Libby and Jazzy after the installation of the dividers. Libby acted more confident and seemed to rub it in the face of her housemate. With secure areas, the cat postured like a queen on her favorite pillow, taunting the puppy spying from the other side of the gate.

In biblical times, whole cities were contained within walls of protection, with gates that could be locked. Citizens of gated communities felt secure and safe, like my Libby. Hedges were used as barriers between neighbors. Job had a hedge of protection around him, placed there by God. What happens when we pray for God to put a hedge around us as well?

Walls are not always divisive. Sometimes they are designed for protection and discipline. A person with boundaries has self-control (empowered by the Holy Spirit). A barrier sometimes makes for good refuge—a safe haven. Libby liked the baby gates, and we can take joy in the refuge created when God builds a wall to protect us.

May the Father of protection place a wall around you to keep you safe and strengthen you to withstand whatever might tempt or harm you. Take joy in the refuge of boundaries.

Grow with Joy

Let's consider how Jesus Christ is a refuge to each of us.

> *But let all who take refuge in you rejoice; let them sing joyful praises forever. Spread your protection over them, that all who love your name may be filled with joy.* (Psalm 5:11)

The word *refuge* means "safe haven, sanctuary, shelter, protection, a place of safety." This psalm suggests all who take refuge in God should do what? Is there any significance to *filled* in this verse?

> *Who will come from Mount Zion to rescue Israel? When the Lord restores his people, Jacob will shout with joy, and Israel will rejoice.* (Psalm 14:7)

We can learn a lot from Israel—the children of God. Sometimes what we learn is what *not* to do. But in this case, we can observe how God's people reacted to being rescued by God. They recognized that any time their nation was rescued or restored, it was an act of God. How can we give God credit for rescuing us, according to this verse?

*Taste and see that the L*ORD *is good. Oh, the joys of those who take refuge in him!* (Psalm 34:8)

Those who take refuge in God experience joy—this we know. How can the first part of the verse help us experience that joy more fully?

*Those who have been ransomed by the L*ORD *will return. They will enter Jerusalem singing, crowned with everlasting joy. Sorrow and mourning will disappear, and they will be filled with joy and gladness.* (Isaiah 51:11)

What from your current life might you list under the category of sorrow or mourning? What is responsible for making you feel trapped or kidnapped against your will?

Imagine God taking all that and paying the ransom price to rescue you. Would this cause you to sing for joy? Isaiah has an interesting turn of phrase, *crowned with everlasting joy.* What does that mean to you?

THE JOY OF REFUGE AND RENEWAL

If we could envision ourselves being rescued, would we experience God any differently than we do now? *Rejoice* is a verb; it means we do something. It's not an emotion we wait to experience. If we are to be joyful, we must focus on the task of getting filled up with joy. Be open to joy—not closed off. Even though we are still learning about this thing called joy, one day we will be crowned with everlasting joy.

> *Rejoice* is a verb; it means we do something. It's not an emotion we wait to experience.

Restore us, O Lord, and bring us back to you again! Give us back the joys we once had. (Lamentations 5:21)

Sometimes we lose our way in this world and need to come back to God. Was there ever a time you felt more joyful in the Lord than you do right now?

If so, what changed? Did you allow something to rob your joy?

Ask the Lord to restore you, and draw close to him again. Joy doesn't stay gone forever when we feel like it disappears; we can discover it again as we allow God to rescue and ransom us.

Go with Joy

Have you ever considered going on an *ask fast*? Essentially, an ask fast is when you set aside a certain amount of time to refrain from asking God for anything. You change all your prayers to focus on the joy of fellowship in his refuge rather than looking at the needs that are so great around you.

Action Steps to Joy

Try some of these steps for your ask fast and see if your joy increases.

1. **Sing praises every morning.** *But as for me, I will sing about your power. Each morning I will sing with joy about your unfailing love. For you have been my refuge, a place of safety when I am in distress* (Psalm 59:16). *I will shout for joy and sing your praises, for you have ransomed me* (Psalm 71:23).

2. **Move in rhythm to praise music during your personal worship time.** Even if you don't dance, consider doing some sort of movement as you worship the Father. A lifting of hands, a march to the beat, tapping your hand on the arm of your chair in time to the music—motion convinces your mind and emotions that you are joyful rather than a victim. *You have turned my mourning into joyful dancing. You have taken away my clothes of mourning and clothed me with joy* (Psalm 30:11).

3. **Find fresh joy in humility.** Change your view of entitlement, and seek to know God more. *The humble will be filled with fresh joy from the LORD. The poor will rejoice in the Holy One of Israel* (Isaiah 29:19).

4. **Put away anger and sadness and put on joy.** *For his anger lasts only a moment, but his favor lasts a lifetime! Weeping may last through the night, but joy comes with the morning* (Psalm 30:5).

Can you think of a time when you were lost as a child? What did it feel like to be found?

THE JOY OF REFUGE AND RENEWAL

Have you ever viewed God as your Rescuer? What did he rescue you from?

Jesus plays the role of Ransom. What price did he pay to buy you back?

The Holy Spirit is our Refuge—our Comforter. Have you ever felt like running away from life? We can run straight into the arms of our refuge. What does God offer in the way of refuge?

Give with Joy

Joy always comes not just in the receiving but in the giving. In today's *Serve It Forward* challenge, may we all consider ways we can offer a little refuge to others. It will bring them joy, but most probably it will bring us joy too.

Serve It Forward in the Joy of Refuge and Renewal

Hurricane Dolly churned over Raymondville, Texas, in 2008. It stalled and camped out on top of us for an extended period of time, and we became acutely aware of the precious security found in safe refuge. We hunkered down at home, just across the street from a city storm shelter, knowing we could go there if conditions worsened. But they wouldn't allow us to bring our fur babies, so we stayed home and watched the storm whip and whirl, all the while dumping inches of rain.

The electricity powered off multiple times—then came back on. Until it didn't. Darkness. The summer heat—suffocating. Dolly's loud whooshing sound grated on every nerve.

Finally . . . silence.

Was it safe to step outside? What would we find? Our home only had minor problems other than pools of water outdoors and debris. We drove through the flooded streets, anticipating what we would find at the church where Russ pastored.

The church! What I first caught sight of caused my heart to sink like an anchor into my belly. The seamed copper roof rolled up like the top of a sardine can, allowing inches of rain to flood the historic sanctuary.

> **This was an opportunity to reach out to our community in its time of need.**

Next we found ourselves in a long car line, waiting for food and water rations. Hot. The entire town without electricity. No air conditioning. No refrigeration. While digging out from under the rubble to determine our next steps we wondered—where would we go from here?

Fortunately our town had no loss of life. But people looked like frightened rabbits. They seemed to be sleepwalking through the motions of survival. Hurricane Dolly's version of post-traumatic stress disorder lasted over a year for many members of our community, and victims had increased health problems from the terrible conditions.

Our home became emergency headquarters, with phone calls, planning meetings, and urgent prayer requests. It was with joy we made our place available for God to use. He inspired us that this was an opportunity to reach out to our community in its time of need.

Our situation could have been much worse. We knew the church was "just a building." But there was something sacred about that historic sanctuary. It knocked the air out of everyone the first time they viewed the destruction. They felt gutted, much like our church looked. Each time I walked someone through the damage reminded me of being at a funeral home, meeting someone at the door who came to the viewing, and walking them up to the casket, sharing good memories of the deceased. We helped members of the congregation gently walk the walk of grief to say their good-byes. To relive their memories one last time. Baby dedications. Salvation decisions. Baptisms. Weddings. Funerals. Every monumental life experience occurred inside those walls. For many, an entire family tree of history was commemorated here. For anyone witnessing the damage, those first moments were sobering—the devastation palpable.

We learned the headaches of dealing with insurance adjusters, contractors, appraisals, demolition, and repairs. Seeing photos of other storm-hit areas didn't prepare us for what barraged all five senses. A foul smell permeated the air from wet ceiling tile and soggy carpet, growing who-knows-what in the heat.

People from all over the country sent us symbols of their love and concern. Donations poured in. Boxes of cleaning supplies and hand sanitizer. And more than material gifts, the support and prayers buoyed us up to experience joy during and after not only the physical storms but the emotional ones, as well.

We scheduled the first of many workdays and planning meetings. People put aside their own storm repairs to help rebuild the church. And the Sunday after the storm, we determined to have a church service, to take communion and thank God for his protection. Despite not having electricity, we met in the hot fellowship hall, away from the primary damage in the sanctuary. The rank conditions couldn't crush the power of community we experienced that day. People were eager to be reassured, to be told everything would be okay—and yet people were willing to sacrifice their own emotional needs to extend love and comfort to others. We met together to show God and the community that he meant more to us than the aftermath of Dolly. We celebrated lives spared, buildings still standing, and that conditions weren't any worse—they could have been much worse. In extreme trials, extreme joy comes from extreme gratitude.

Russ ended his first post-Dolly sermon with this quote by Viktor Frankl, concentration camp survivor: "Everything can be taken from a man but one thing: to choose one's attitude in any given set of circumstances, to choose one's way."

> **In extreme trials, extreme joy comes from extreme gratitude.**

Since Hurricane Dolly, I've endured several more hurricanes and tropical storms. While the conditions never get easier, the opportunity for serving up joy never diminishes.

How might you serve it forward to help others experience the joy of refuge and renewal?

Your Grin-with-Joy Challenge

You have felt buried under the weight of obligations and relationship drama for a while. You just want to run away from your problems and hide. If only you could block out the demanding noise—like kids who stick their fingers in their ears and sing, "La la la, I can't hear you!" In your daily Bible reading, you discover there is one place where you can run for refuge and renewal. What do you do next to seek God with renewed joy?

Chapter Seven

THE *Joy* OF WISDOM

Joy is the flag you fly when the Prince of Peace is in residence within your heart. —Wilfred Peterson

God gives his children the ability to process knowledge through discernment, which results in great wisdom. As we gain his insights, our joy increases. And when we make choices based on his wisdom, we please God. Our joy grows as he delights in us.

Grin with Joy

Have you ever had one of those brain-fry moments when nothing new can be learned or decided upon and nothing old can be recalled? Sometimes I pray aloud, "Lord, I'm over fifty, and I know you can teach an old dog new tricks, but I do need a little extra assistance!"

What do you do when you feel like you've hit the wall and you can't focus on any more tasks? Do you allow yourself time for a diversion? Watch mindless television? Take a walk or a bath and zone out? How do you free some space in your mind's hard drive so you can function with greater speed and ability?

I could write a magazine article from what I've learned and title it "Top Seven Ways to Improve Brain Power."

1. Get plenty of sleep.
2. Eat whole foods.
3. Deal with stress in positive ways.
4. Surround yourself with a good support system.
5. Remove negative distracters from your life.
6. Delegate tasks to others.
7. Discover which hours are your brain-surge hours and do your most difficult mental tasks during that time period.

Right now I'm taking a breather. Sometimes just changing gears by focusing on a different task helps. But I've also taken the time to pray and ask God to assist me. I know I can't do it on my own. The Bible says if any lack wisdom, we just need to ask for it (James 1:5). Ask for it I will! This isn't a request for any old wisdom, but for godly wisdom.

The next time you feel overwhelmed and can't focus, take a five-minute mini vacation and visit the throne room of God. There's nothing like talking to royalty to put things in perspective.

Exercise What?

Exercising can be a great time to clear our minds and have alone time—vital to refreshing our focus. Not only does fitness training help us to lose weight and tone up, it has other health benefits too, and it gives us a "natural high" due to the release of endorphins.

But there is something more important than physical exercise. First Timothy 1:8 says physical exercise profits little (it does profit though!). Then it goes on to say that godliness is profitable to all things.

How does someone strive for godliness? Since the Bible compares this to physical exercise, then it must take work! Part of this exercise is choosing to seek the things of God and the mind of God. Bible reading and prayer are musts, but it goes further than that. Becoming godly is a process that stimulates growth as we have an active, intimate relationship with God. Only when we involve him in every aspect of our lives can we live devoted to him.

A godly person isn't distracted by the glitter of the world and has a sole desire to please God. She makes choices based on what would honor God, and she has wisdom based on God's Word. She is in tune with the Holy Spirit's leadership in her life. A godly person determines to live a holy life even when that life isn't easy. When I think of choosing role models for my life, my first priority is for them to be godly.

> We can do this! None of us wants a flabby mind (or flabby arms for that matter)!

There is another form of exercise. First Peter 1:13 says, *Therefore gird up the loins of your mind, be sober, and rest your hope fully upon the grace that is to be brought to you at the revelation of Jesus Christ* (NKJV). In other words, work hard so you don't have a flabby mind! We are to prepare our minds for action. The imagery here is that of personal discipline and outward conduct.

We can do this! None of us wants a flabby mind (or flabby arms for that matter)!

Grow with Joy

What do you think are the basic differences between knowledge, wisdom, and understanding?

- **Knowledge.** The collection of information and facts acquired through education or experience. Knowledge is only as good as its source. For example, growing in the knowledge of our Lord is a good thing, but accumulating knowledge from a professor who isn't a believer might lead a person down the wrong path.

- **Wisdom.** Good sense to know the truth about the accumulation of facts. Having sound judgment based on knowledge. The ability to discern. Wisdom chooses whether or not to act on what we know. Wisdom plus the direction of the Holy Spirit leads to understanding.
- **Understanding.** Discernment to know what to do with wisdom, which leads to godly behavior that pleases our heavenly Father. A person with understanding is able to comprehend what they know and are able to make wise choices with that knowledge. We develop understanding when we put our beliefs (knowledge and wisdom) into practice.

For wisdom will enter your heart, and knowledge will fill you with joy. (Proverbs 2:10)

Joyful is the person who finds wisdom, the one who gains understanding. (Proverbs 3:13)

According to these verses, what fills us with joy?

God gives wisdom, knowledge, and joy to those who please him. (Ecclesiastes 2:26)

To whom does God give wisdom, knowledge, and joy?

So if you want wisdom, knowledge, and joy, what do you need to do?

A wise child brings joy to a father; a foolish child brings grief to a mother. (Proverbs 10:1)

The father of godly children has cause for joy. What a pleasure to have children who are wise. (Proverbs 23:24)

Parents are filled with joy and good pleasure when their children act in wisdom. How can we bring joy and good pleasure to our heavenly Father?

Go with Joy

If joy comes with wisdom, how does a person go about getting wisdom? The Bible gives many principles when it comes to this, which we will incorporate into this chapter's *Action Steps to Joy*.

Action Steps to Joy

1. **Desire wisdom with your whole being.** Esteem it as something of great value. *If you prize wisdom, she will make you great. Embrace her, and she will honor you* (Proverbs 4:8).

2. **Study and meditate on Scripture, since wisdom is found in the Word of God.** Devote yourself to learning all you can about the Bible, by reading it and also reading books by wise Christians who expound on biblical truths. *The instructions of the L<small>ORD</small> are perfect, reviving the soul. The decrees of the L<small>ORD</small> are trustworthy, making wise the simple* (Psalm 19:7).

3. **Pray for wisdom.** We have a source for more wisdom, so we have no excuse. We can't say, "But I'm just not wise. I wasn't born that way, and I can't seem to figure out how to get more wisdom." God wants to increase our wisdom: *So we have not stopped praying for you since we first heard about you. We ask God to give you complete knowledge of his will and to give you spiritual wisdom and understanding* (Colossians 1:9). *Asking God, the glorious Father of our Lord Jesus Christ, to give you spiritual wisdom and insight so that you might grow*

in your knowledge of God (Ephesians 1:17). *If you need wisdom, ask our generous God, and he will give it to you. He will not rebuke you for asking* (James 1:5).

4. **Keep in perspective that life on earth is short; it's time to seek wisdom now.** Don't put it off! *Teach us to realize the brevity of life, so that we may grow in wisdom* (Psalm 90:12).

5. **Draw near to God, and be filled with his wisdom.** *In him lie hidden all the treasures of wisdom and knowledge* (Colossians 2:3).

Think of a time this past week when you've needed more wisdom. What did you do about it?

How do joy and wisdom go hand in hand?

What is one action step in this chapter that you want to implement this coming week so you don't feel stuck or paralyzed the next time you need more wisdom?

Give with Joy

Whenever we settle into a new home, I select a place of honor for one of our heirlooms. It is a framed charcoal drawing of one of my husband's ancestors. The name on the back of the picture is James Spilvin Willis. This rendering of Great-Great-Grandfather Willis reminds me of the painting of Mona Lisa. He is not smiling, and his eyes seem to follow me around the room!

He wears a dark suit with a high-cut vest and a white shirt with no tie. His face sports a scruffy goatee but no mustache. His hair is clipped short. He reminds me of a circuit preacher. I wanted to find out more about this forefather of ours.

I researched and learned that Great-Great-Grandfather Willis was born in 1837 and lived until 1881, dying at the age of forty-three. His father's name was Noah, and I discovered the names of his six children, as well. Martin Luther Willis, who lived eighty-two years, fathered my husband's grandfather. I can't help but wonder, with the biblical name of Noah for James' father, and since he named his own son Martin Luther, if the man in this picture hanging on my wall was a preacher just like his great-great-grandson.

> I hope to have those who follow me attribute their spiritual walk, in part, to the influence I've had in their lives.

I go into all this detail to share this thought: it is good to learn about and be thankful for our forefathers. We are shaped by how our families before us lived—and not just our blood relatives. Many of us have Christian brothers and sisters who have taken the time to mentor us. Think about who shared Christ with you . . . and who shared Christ with that person. You could almost trace it back, much like a family tree.

But the most important aspect of this family tree is that we bear fruit as Christians and form new branches. I hope to have those who follow me attribute their spiritual walk, in part, to the influence I've had in their lives, and I'm sure you do too. What are you doing now to see the tree of Christian life continue to grow and multiply?

Our mentors instill in us knowledge, wisdom, and understanding. Thank the ones who have impacted your life while you still have time. And pray for God to show you the name of someone into whom you can pour your own life. We have no choice about impacting others; we only have the choice of whether we are impacting them for the good or for the bad. How does your Christian family tree look today?

Serve It Forward in the Joy of Wisdom

One way we can mentor others as they grow in their Christian walk is to help them discern God's wisdom. We help them put wisdom into practice by showing them how we think God is leading and guiding. It's up to us to be there for them when they ask, "How do I gain godly wisdom as opposed to earthly wisdom?" The Bible says it is wise to surround ourselves with wise counselors (Proverbs 11:14). That's true. But let's take it one step further and be willing to be part of a supportive wisdom team for others. God will show you the ones he wants you to mentor. This is part of biblical discipleship—training others to grow in the knowledge of the Lord. As you serve it forward, ask God to show you wisdom and then be willing to share your insights and input with others. As we help shine the light on his truth, we all experience more of the peace of God that surpasses all human understanding.

Your Grin-with-Joy Challenge

One of your favorite women's magazines mentions the idea of finding and being a mentor. Then you turn on the radio, and the host is interviewing a mentoring expert. Then a friend gives you a book she just finished, and—you guessed it—it's about mentoring. You like the idea of being a mentor and having a mentor, but how do you go about finding the right people? After you pray for direction and wisdom, what is your first step to finding joy through mentoring?

Chapter Eight

THE FULLNESS OF *Joy*

It is his joy that remains in us that makes
our joy full. —A. B. SIMPSON

As the joy of the Lord fills us, we are moved to worship him, surrendered completely. This joy increases as we focus on his attributes and good works. In the presence of his majesty, we experience the awe of joyful adoration.

Grin with Joy

Julie selects her clothes the night before, and lays them out in the guest bedroom, shoes at the foot of the bed to complete the outfit. Tracy asks hubby to set the alarm for 6:00 a.m., and then rechecks the alarm clock herself, just to be safe. Sherrie tosses and turns in bed all night, seeing every hour click by on the clock. Anticipation gets the best of her, so she arises early to prepare for the day.

What day, you ask? A child's first day of school? No. Perhaps Christmas morning? No. A first day of work? No, that's not it either. The answer? The day after Thanksgiving.

"What!" you may ask. "How can it be?"

Never underestimate the determination of a woman in search of a good sale!

But this does cause me to wonder: why is it that we barely have the energy to drag out of bed to go to work, and we seem to think church services are entirely too early, but we can bound out of bed when we anticipate shopping for bargains?

> When I realize that all my tasks, even the menial ones, please God when I do them with all my heart, I will jump out of bed with joy.

Maybe you are not a shopper. But I'm certain there is still one special event that causes you to wake up eagerly. For you, it could be the day your baby will make his appearance, neighborhood garage sale day or the first day of vacation.

My prayer is that I will be more of a morning person, that I will greet every day as if it were a day I highly anticipated. No matter what is on my schedule for the day, it is the day the Lord has made. How can I start the day with joy rather than drag my feet? The only way I know how is to apply this verse from Colossians: *Whatever you do, work heartily, as for the Lord and not for men* (3:23 ESV). When I realize that all my tasks, even the menial ones, please God when I do them with all my heart, I will jump out of bed with joy.

The next time you grumble when the alarm clock rings, embrace the day, and God will energize you to spring out of bed rather than slap the snooze button. Certainly if we start the day with joy, anticipating good things ahead, we will experience the fullness of joy all day long.

Full Up!

Dad unbuckled his belt. It wasn't bedtime—he wasn't undressing. But I knew I wasn't in trouble. Instead, *he* was in trouble. He'd eaten too much again. Mom is a terrific cook. It is a common problem to pull away from the table feeling nearly miserable—unable to eat another bite. I used to think older men were goofy, the way they'd lose all sense of decorum and loosen their waistbands like that.

Eating at Granny's was a similar experience, only then we had several men seated around the family table with bellies swollen from "healthy" appetites. Uncle Eddie often tipped his chair back like he was doing a wheelie, something for which we'd get in trouble at home. He'd start in on a story, often punctuating the exciting parts with exaggeration accented by his southern drawl. And almost always at some point, the best compliment we'd all give Granny would be another southern expression: "I'm full up!" This announcement was usually accompanied by the obligatory belly rub, like we were trying to put our organs back into their proper positions. (Imagine Andy Griffith after one of Aunt Bea's meals, and you capture the scene.)

Now that I'm older, I find myself wishing for a looser waistband after mealtime too. I understand the grown-ups. We're more like grown-outs. Or groan-outs!

These *full-up* mealtimes were (and still are) the best though! Good food. And even better? Creating memorable family times.

God wants to fill us up in such a way that our joy overflows. Then we rub our hearts as we proclaim, "I'm full up!"

Grow with Joy

The Bible accounts many times when believers worshipped in joy.

> *They all went to Gilgal, and in a solemn ceremony before the* Lord *they made Saul king. Then they offered peace offerings to the* Lord, *and Saul and all the Israelites were filled with joy.* (1 Samuel 11:15)

Why do you think Saul and all the Israelites were filled with joy? Notice what actions they took leading up to this experience. What can you gain from this inspiration to help you be filled with joy?

> *Honor and majesty surround him; strength and joy fill his dwelling.* (1 Chronicles 16:27)

Him in this verse refers to God. So replace *him* with *God* and reread the statement. What surrounds God? What accompanies joy in filling his dwelling?

We are to emulate our Lord. What can we take from this verse to use as a pattern in our lives?

> *The people rejoiced over the offerings, for they had given freely and wholeheartedly to the LORD, and King David was filled with joy.* (1 Chronicles 29:9)

Leaders are filled with joy when their followers give freely and wholeheartedly. In this verse, the people blessed David by how they gave to the Lord. When considering your offerings to the Lord (resources, finances, talents, etc.), how might you give with more joy, and how might that spirit of giving bless the Lord as well as his leaders?

> *But let the godly rejoice. Let them be glad in God's presence. Let them be filled with joy.* (Psalm 68:3)

I find the word *let* an interesting choice of words here. It is used three times in three sentences, so it must be important. It's almost like a proclamation, as in "Let the games begin!" It is way of celebrating the initiation of something anticipated.

THE FULLNESS OF JOY

The godly will:

- Rejoice.
- Be glad.
- Be in God's presence.
- Be filled with joy.

> *But may all who search for you be filled with joy and gladness in you. May those who love your salvation repeatedly shout, "God is great!"* (Psalm 70:4)

May is another word of proclamation, like *let*. *You* in this verse refers to God. These sentences are worded like if/then conditional phrases: if you do this, then you get this in return.

If you:

- Search for God, may you be _____ .
- Love your salvation, may you _____ .

A sign of being filled with joy and gladness is to feel like shouting "God is great!" repeatedly.

> *When they saw the star, they were filled with joy!* (Matthew 2:10)

The wise men noticed a new star in the sky and understood what it meant. They came to Jerusalem to find Jesus and worship him. After King Herod sent them on to Bethlehem, the star led them to the house where Jesus was. Why do you think they were filled with joy when they saw the star again?

I can't see how they could have had ordinary lives after their intersection with the star and the Christ child. What affect does it have on you when you see signs of Jesus in your everyday life?

When Jesus intersected your life, did it make a life-changing difference in your level of joy?

When he arrived and saw this evidence of God's blessing, he was filled with joy, and he encouraged the believers to stay true to the Lord. (Acts 11:23)

God equips us to be filled with joy when we're filled with the Spirit.

He in this verse is Barnabas, a good man with strong faith and a wonderful way of encouraging others in the Lord. This visit took place after Stephen's terrible stoning. Believers in Antioch were preaching the gospel to the Gentiles there. The church in Jerusalem sent Barnabas to see how they were doing. According to this verse, Barnabas was pleased with what he observed. We learn from this example that when we witness God's blessing in others, we will be filled with joy. Like Barnabas, I want to not only be joy-filled, but encourage others to stay true to God.

Filled with the Spirit

God equips us to be filled with joy when we're filled with the Spirit. There's nothing magical or mystical about this; it's simply 100% God and 0% self at any given time. All other equations mean there's a vacancy for God's activity in us. If you remember a time when you felt closer to the Lord than now, it's probably because you were more yielded to the Spirit at that point in your life. He was your number one priority. Perhaps he is your main focus right now. But if your joy isn't quite full, it's possible you aren't fully yielded to the Holy Spirit. It might be a symptom that you're holding something back.

Here are a few Scriptures about being filled with the Spirit: *Look, I have specifically chosen Bezalel son of Uri, grandson of Hur, of the tribe of Judah. I have filled him with the Spirit of God, giving him great wisdom, ability, and expertise in all kinds of crafts* (Exodus 31:2–3). *But as for me, I am filled with power—with the Spirit of the LORD. I am filled with justice and strength to boldly declare Israel's sin and rebellion* (Micah 3:8). *Don't be drunk with wine, because that will ruin your life. Instead, be filled with the Holy Spirit, singing psalms and hymns and spiritual songs among yourselves, and making music to the Lord in your hearts* (Ephesians 5:18–19).

Go with Joy

When I received a diabetes diagnosis I realized it was time for change. I had no choice but to learn a new way of life, a routine that encompassed healthy eating, exercise, finger pricks for blood glucose readings, reducing stress, and more. When I set those goals as New Year's resolutions, I realized most adults set similar goals even if they don't have diabetes: healthy eating, exercise, and reducing stress. We all know it is best if we eat less, move more, and destress.

> I believe in embracing all things with gratitude, even if it starts out as an exercise rather than a welcome emotion.

I believe in embracing all things with gratitude, even if it starts out as an exercise rather than a welcome emotion. Sometimes the discipline of counting my blessings even when I don't feel like it helps me have a more positive approach—a better perspective. The new-and-improved outlook helps me accept the inevitable without digging my heels into the ground in stubborn rebellion.

Perhaps my personal gratitude list of why I'm glad I have diabetes will inspire your own gratitude list as you seek to have a new attitude about something in your life. Pick something unpleasant going on in your life and make it more bearable by finding the good in it.

Why I'm glad I have diabetes:

1. A diabetic diet is a healthy way of eating.
2. I will lose the excess weight as I make healthier food choices.
3. I will heal better after procedures and surgeries when my blood glucose levels are under control.
4. I'm less tempted to make unhealthy eating choices because I have an eating plan.
5. I will be more understanding of what other diabetics go through.
6. By catching it early, I avoid or delay some of the long-term effects of the disease.
7. I will become physically fit as I follow a disciplined exercise plan.
8. I'm allowed to eat a variety of foods within my appetites and cravings.
9. I will save money on groceries and restaurant bills as my portion sizes decrease.
10. When my body reaches a healthier status, I will feel better, which will then affect my spiritual and emotional health as well.

The old standby advice for how to eat an elephant is one bite at a time. This is also the best advice for dealing with any problem—just take it one bite, one step, at a time.

Ask God to help you overcome one seemingly insurmountable problem as we learn to grin with joy. Allow him to help you view the problem from a different perspective. Break down the issues, one bite at a time. You can swallow anything if the bites are small enough. Before you know it, you will have victory over your trial. Start with exercising the right choices, which leads to the right attitude, and entrust the circumstances to God. He will give you enough grace to cope with any of life's many unpleasant situations. And in the end, that gratitude list might evolve from an exercise of the will to abundant joy!

Action Steps to Joy

"Joy springs from within; no one makes you joyous; you choose joyfulness."—Unknown.

1. **Search for God.** *But may all who search for you be filled with joy and gladness in you. May those who love your salvation repeatedly shout, "The Lord is great!"* (Psalm 40:16).
2. **Practice the presence of God.** Sense his nearness in your everyday life. *You have shown me the way of life, and you will fill me with the joy of your presence* (Acts 2:28).

3. **Be filled with the Holy Spirit.** *And the believers were filled with joy and with the Holy Spirit* (Acts 13:52).
4. **Rejoice in the Lord.** *Always be full of joy in the Lord. I say it again—rejoice!* (Philippians 4:4).

Discuss what being full of joy, or *fullness of joy*, feels like.

Has there ever been a time when you felt closer to the Lord than right now? What changed?

What needs to change to improve your intimacy with him?

If being filled with joy begins with being filled with the Spirit, is there anything you need to subtract or add to your life to pursue a Spirit-filled *and* joy-filled life?

How might a change in your perspective change your joy level?

Give with Joy

People often confuse happiness and joy. They get stuck in the trap of "If only . . ." Some popular "If only . . ." statements include:

- If only my husband hadn't filed for divorce, I'd be happy.
- If only I could lose twenty pounds, I'd be happy.
- If only my children wouldn't cause me so much heartache, I'd be happy.
- If only I'd get a pay raise, I'd be happy.
- If only I didn't have this disease, I'd be happy.
- If only I could have children, I'd be happy.
- If only I had a mate, I'd be happy.

What's the danger of "If only . . ." statements? If you depend on something outside your control for your joy, you will be discouraged and depressed often. If your source of joy is your relationship with God, you will have fullness of joy even when circumstances aren't joyous.

Happiness comes and goes depending on its fancy or whim; joy wants to be a permanent resident.

> Happiness comes and goes depending on its fancy or whim; joy wants to be a permanent resident.

Serve It Forward in the Fullness of Joy

One way to serve it forward is to help another person make the switch from pursuing happiness based on circumstances to pursuing joy that stays put even when good times are absent. How might you help an "If only . . ." person make this change?

We can teach others through being an example and by coming alongside and providing good advice. Of course, it's always a good thing to make sure people are ready to receive, or the life lessons won't make a difference in their lives.

Life Lessons for Pursuing Joy

Help someone burdened with discouragement or depression develop an action plan for growing more joyful. Here are some ideas to get you started.

- Focus on God's blessings and his answers to prayer. Reject negative thinking and replace it with thoughts that lead to contentment.
- Don't wait for good news to experience the fullness of joy. Practice joy in the midst of a trial.
- Put God to the test. God doesn't need you to have even one good thing going on in life for you to be joyful. Rejoice and see that the Lord is good!

- Replace "If only . . ." statements with "God is enough" statements. Not "If only God would bless me with a job promotion—then I would be joyful." Instead: "Even if I don't get that job promotion, God is enough for me to experience joy."
- Consider reading *Happiness Is a Choice* by Dr. Frank Minirth and Dr. Paul Meier.

Don't worry about anything; instead, pray about everything. Tell God what you need, and thank him for all he has done. Then you will experience God's peace, which exceeds anything we can understand. His peace will guard your hearts and minds as you live in Christ Jesus. And now, dear brothers and sisters, one final thing. Fix your thoughts on what is true, and honorable, and right, and pure, and lovely, and admirable. Think about things that are excellent and worthy of praise. Keep putting into practice all you learned and received from me—everything you heard from me and saw me doing. Then the God of peace will be with you. (Philippians 4:6–9)

Fix your thoughts on what is:

- T_____
- H_____
- R_____
- P_____
- L_____
- A_____
- E_____
- W_____ of P_____

Your Grin-with-Joy Challenge

You notice a big change in one of your friends. It's as if joy is spilling out of her heart and splashing on everyone she touches. You want that kind of joy and ask her to reveal her secret. She says it's all about being filled with the Spirit—100% God and 0% you. Surrendering everything as an act of worship. You want fullness of joy like that. How do you go about offering yourself as an act of worship to the Father?

Chapter Nine

THE SONGS OF *Joy*

> We may sing beforehand, even in our winter storm, in the expectation of a summer sun at the turn of the year; no created powers can mar our Lord Jesus' music, nor spill our song of joy. Let us then be glad and rejoice in the salvation of our Lord; for faith has never yet cause to have wet cheeks, and hanging-down brows, or to droop or die. —SAMUEL RUTHERFORD

The Lord's goodness leads us to worship him in song. Our posture acknowledges his lordship, and our mouths praise his name. We shout for joy as we seek his face and experience his blessings. Music fills the air and joy fills each heart.

Grin with Joy

When I sing of Christ's beauty, the words draw me in to imagine just how beautiful Jesus must have been while on this earth, and how beautiful he is to me today. And when I am drawn to beautiful Christians, it is their radiant glow (which reflects the beauty of Christ) that attracts me.

Physical features fade in comparison. I want to be with people who cherish the Lord in a personal way. Joy is evident on their countenances.

I think this is what also draws me to Jesus. He is the one who can bring me to the Father. While on this earth, he was completely focused on the Father's will for his life. He knew what his purpose was—his special design. I gravitate toward believers who know what God wants for their lives, those willing to sacrifice everything else in pursuit of godly direction.

How beautiful is the sweet glow of mercy on the face of Jesus. How special are the arms held open wide, to welcome me to his side. How piercing are his eyes, penetrating me with his love and understanding. His mouth shares both laughter and smiles of contentment. His words beckon me.

> I gravitate toward believers who know what God wants for their lives, those willing to sacrifice everything else in pursuit of godly direction.

I desire to worship Jesus in all of his beauty. We often forget how to truly worship. Or perhaps you never learned how. May we make our adoration known to him, singing songs of joy based on who he is and who we are when we are with him. We must not hold back for fear of intimacy! Only when we are drawn to him can we know him. When we are drawn to new friends in Christ, we must drop our walls of inhibition to really know and be known of them. Equally so, when we seek Jesus, we must throw aside any weight that slows us down or holds us back, and run to him.

I can scarcely fathom what it will be like when I see my Savior face to face. How overjoyed will I be, yet how humbled! I am determined not to wait for my heavenly graduation to worship Jesus: *Happy are those who hear the joyful call to worship, for they will walk in the light of your presence,* LORD (Psalm 89:15).

I Forgot the Words!

Have you ever had this problem before? I'll be singing along with some of my favorite Christian music artists, and all of a sudden, they'll change the words on me! How in the world could they write a song, record the song, sing the song as part of their career—and then go and get the words wrong? Oh—you mean it was I who messed up?

No worries! Somehow those songs still do a number on me, even when I forget the words. (Okay, I admit it. I absolutely *destroy* lyrics!) There's something about the music that makes me feel more joyful. Add in lyrics that help me focus on my relationship with the Lord, and that's a recipe for joyfulness.

Singing songs of joy leads to an increased joy perspective. It doesn't have to be on a stage in front of a spotlight. Sing in your car, in your shower, as you do housework. Just sing. Try it. You'll like the joy it produces—even if you forget the words!

Oh for a Thousand Tongues to Sing
Lyrics, Charles Wesley, 1739

O for a thousand tongues to sing
My great Redeemer's praise,
The glories of my God and King,
The triumphs of his grace!

My gracious Master and my God,
Assist me to proclaim,
To spread through all the earth abroad
The honors of Thy name.

Jesus! the name that charms our fears,
That bids our sorrows cease;
'Tis music in the sinner's ears,
'Tis life, and health, and peace.

He breaks the power of canceled sin,
He sets the prisoner free;
His blood can make the foulest clean,
His blood availed for me.

He speaks, and, listening to his voice,
New life the dead receive,
The mournful, broken hearts rejoice,
The humble poor believe.

Hear Him, ye deaf; his praise, ye dumb,
Your loosened tongues employ;
Ye blind, behold your Savior come,
And leap, ye lame, for joy.

In Christ your Head, you then shall know,
Shall feel your sins forgiven;

> Anticipate your heaven below,
> And own that love is heaven.
>
> Sudden expired the legal strife,
> 'Twas then I ceased to grieve;
> My second, real, living life
> I then began to live.

Grow with Joy

The believers in the Bible provide wonderful examples for how songs and other acts of worship lead to joy.

Fire blazed forth from the Lord's presence and consumed the burnt offering and the fat on the altar. When the people saw this, they shouted with joy and fell face down on the ground. (Leviticus 9:24)

Why did the people worship the Lord, according to this passage in Leviticus?

Have you ever tried a new worship posture, such as being prone, with face down on the ground? Why might that position enhance your worship experience? How might it distract?

THE SONGS OF JOY

> *When all the Israelites saw the Ark of the Covenant of the L*ORD *coming into the camp, their shout of joy was so loud it made the ground shake!* (1 Samuel 4:5)

Put yourself in this scenario. What did the ark represent to the Israelites?

Why did it stir up such an outburst of joyful worship when they observed the Ark of the Covenant coming back to their camp?

> *David and all the people of Israel brought up the Ark of the L*ORD *with shouts of joy and the blowing of rams' horns.* (2 Samuel 6:15)

> *All Israel brought up the Ark of the L*ORD*'s Covenant with shouts of joy, the blowing of rams' horns and trumpets, the crashing of cymbals, and loud playing on harps and lyres.* (1 Chronicles 15:28)

> *Sing your praise to the L*ORD *with the harp, . . . with trumpets and the sound of the ram's horn. Make a joyful symphony before the L*ORD*, the King!* (Psalm 98:5–6)

According to the *Jewish Encyclopaedia*, the curved ram's horn (a shofar) is symbolic of the contrite heart: sorry, remorseful, repentant, regretful. The shofar represents the windpipe that moves our breath, it inhales and exhales, symbolic of the spiritual aspect of a person. This is in contrast to the esophagus right next to it, which signifies the physical aspect of a person—it transports food to nourish the body. The sound of the shofar awakens the Higher Mercy.

Knowing the history of the ram's horn, how does blowing it and shouting with joy create an element of rejoicing and worship?

All the people followed Solomon into Jerusalem, playing flutes and shouting for joy. The celebration was so joyous and noisy that the earth shook with the sound. (1 Kings 1:40)

Doesn't this sound like a parade? Recall some of the joyful features of your favorite parade. How might you add that same spirit of joy to your worship time, whether alone or in a group?

Many of the older priests, Levites, and other leaders who had seen the first Temple wept aloud when they saw the new Temple's foundation. The others, however, were shouting for joy. (Ezra 3:12)

Worship brings about different emotions for different individuals. Some cry, some shout for joy. Think of a worship moment when you felt God's presence intimately—were you more likely to cry or experience another joyful expression?

I long, yes, I faint with longing to enter the courts of the LORD. With my whole being, body and soul, I will shout joyfully to the living God. (Psalm 84:2)

When Russ and I had dated a while, we started to get serious, and I started to get sick! Russ experienced the same symptoms. At first, we wondered if it might be mono. (No—not because of it being the "kissing disease"!) One day, Russ's mom figured out what was wrong with us. We were *lovesick*. She said this was a classic case of falling in love—we had all the signs. Have you ever felt physical symptoms in your worship of the Lord? Describe what it must mean to long so much for God that you feel faint.

When your entire being is focused on joyfully worshipping the Lord, you might experience lovesickness. It's the ache of homesickness that misses a *person* rather than a place.

I will be filled with joy because of you. I will sing praises to your name, O Most High. (Psalm 9:2)

So often we say we will be joyful if something happens. This verse strips all the conditions for happiness away and shows us how simple joy is. When joy is absent from your heart and mind, consider making a similar statement: "I choose to be filled with joy *because of You, God.*" It's all because of him. Every bit of it. And that fullness of joy leads us to want to sing praises to his name. If you don't feel like singing, is joy the delight of your life or has joy departed your life?

Let the godly sing for joy to the Lord; it is fitting for the pure to praise him. (Psalm 33:1)

Look who sings for joy to the Lord—the godly. And for whom is it fitting to praise him? The pure. This is another verse that provides a good checkup for us if we don't feel like singing for joy. If joy is missing, look to see if you're striving to live a godly life and if you are disciplined to be pure of mind and body. When we make it a priority to pattern our lives after a righteous and holy God, we can experience an increase in joyous praise as we sing to him (and sing *because* of him).

> **When we make it a priority to pattern our lives after a righteous and holy God, we can experience an increase in joyous praise as we sing to him.**

Because you are my helper, I sing for joy in the shadow of your wings. (Psalm 63:7)

Why did the psalmist sing for joy?

THE SONGS OF JOY

How is God our helper? Some versions of the Bible even translate the word *Comforter* (the Holy Spirit) as *Helper.*

Where did the psalmist sing for joy?

What do you think it means to be in the shadow of God's wings? How might that cause joy to be stirred up in the singer?

> *Let the whole world sing for joy, because you govern the nations with justice and guide the people of the whole world.* (Psalm 67:4)

Somehow when I read this verse, I picture a certain soda commercial where Bohemian-type singers hold hands and sing, "What the world needs now is love, sweet love." I'm pretty certain what the world needs now is to acknowledge and submit to the love of the Father, who is sovereign (in kingly control) above all else. Can you imagine the day when the whole world of believers will sing for joy because of God's works and his attributes? What a day that will be!

> *I think of the good old days, long since ended, when my nights were filled with joyful songs. I search my soul and ponder the difference now.* (Psalm 77:5–6)

We all have times we are awake when we should be asleep. Perhaps rather than our reaching for a boring book or a sleeping pill, God would prefer to hear the sound of our joyful songs. Dr. Charles Page says God allows us to be sleepless to spend time with us every once in a while. Whether we can't sleep because our minds are racing with so many good things or burdened by so much stress—singing praises to God will help. Interesting second sentence in this verse: when I can't sleep, it's a good time for me to search my soul and consider the difference God can make in my life when I let him.

Go with Joy

> "It's better to shout than to doubt
> It's better to rise than to fall,
> It's better to let the glory out
> Than to have no glory at all."
>
> —Early Student Volunteers, England
> (Quote from: *Jesus, Man of Joy* by Sherwood Eliot Wirt)

The phrases, *Shout to the Lord* and *Shout with joy* are often used when discussing worship. What is the significance of the word *shout* when it comes to joyful worship? In traditional church services, sometimes there's a concern of being proper and decent more than the practice of shouting as an expression of joy. We'd rather be accused of being polite than being out of control. And there *is* something to be said for conducting church services *decently and in order* (1 Corinthians 14:40 KJV).

THE SONGS OF JOY

A raised voice shouts "Hallelujah!" or "Amen!" A song of praise or a clap of hands lifts the rafters along with raising the volume. Joy can cause spontaneous eruptions of sound. Joy-filled worship is deeply personal and as unique as a fingerprint. There is no one way to express joy. And there is a balancing act. We wouldn't want to distract from the group's worship experience, but we don't want to be so concerned with what others think that we limit our worship. That only serves to put the object of our concern in a higher place of exaltation than our Lord.

> Joy-filled worship is deeply personal and as unique as a fingerprint.

More "shouting verses":

- *How the king rejoices in your strength, O LORD! He shouts with joy because you give him victory.* (Psalm 21:1)
- *Come, everyone! Clap your hands! Shout to God with joyful praise!* (Psalm 47:1)
- *Those who live at the ends of the earth stand in awe of your wonders. From where the sun rises to where it sets, you inspire shouts of joy.* (Psalm 65:8)
- *Shout to the LORD, all the earth; break out in praise and sing for joy!* (Psalm 98:4)
- *Come, let us sing to the LORD! Let us shout joyfully to the Rock of our salvation.* (Psalm 95:1)
- *Rejoice in the LORD and be glad, all you who obey him! Shout for joy, all you whose hearts are pure!* (Psalm 32:11)
- *I will hold my head high above my enemies who surround me. At his sanctuary I will offer sacrifices with shouts of joy, singing and praising the LORD with music.* (Psalm 27:6)

Action Steps to Joy

What will you do to grow in joy through your personal worship time? Here are a few ideas to get you started.

1. **Praise God for answered prayers and God's provision.** *May we shout for joy when we hear of your victory and raise a victory banner in the name of our God. May the LORD answer all your prayers"* (Psalm 20:5).
2. **Learn a new worship song.** Focus on the words. Tap in to your joy as you sing. *Sing a new song of praise to him; play skillfully on the harp, and sing with joy* (Psalm 33:3).
3. **Sing a song thanking God for his work in your world.** *Let them offer sacrifices of thanksgiving and sing joyfully about his glorious acts* (Psalm 107:22).

4. **Focus on how God satisfies you.** This will lead to joyful songs of praise. *You satisfy me more than the richest feast. I will praise you with songs of joy* (Psalm 63:5).

5. **Even in your down times and bedtimes, be joyful as you sing about how good God is to you.** *Let the faithful rejoice that he honors them. Let them sing for joy as they lie on their beds* (Psalm 149:5).

Why do you think music is such an important part of joy?

What can you do to insert more music into your day?

Is there anything you can add to your Sunday worship to get more joy out of the group experience?

How important are the words as you use songs to express your worship and joy? How important is the tune? What works for you, and what doesn't work as well?

How open are you to trying new styles of worship and worship music? Or do familiar songs bring more joy?

Give with Joy

While attending a sacred music conference in San Antonio, I contemplated the definition of worship. We heard every style of Christian music available today, including Southern gospel, urban gospel, octavos, and praise and worship—we sampled it all! We especially enjoyed a singing group named This Hope, who sang a unique blend of a cappella and accompanied music. Their tight harmonies gave a fresh take on old favorites. Because their music was energetic and uplifting, we left feeling physically lighter, as if there was less gravity keeping us in touch with the earth—something only music can do.

My favorite segment of the conference was when songwriters introduced their new pieces. They led us in sight-reading the music or conducted a choir in a sample performance. I wonder if that might be the closest comparison these composers have to experiencing childbirth? They conceived the lyrics or the music in their hearts before it ever moved to their heads and then out of their lips or instruments, eventually appearing on the printed page and then sung by others—the birth of a musical piece!

Music is one of many tools of worship. God created all our senses to praise and glorify him. Sight is another phenomenal source of inspiration for worship. What we see can lead us to bow the knee, or at least bow our hearts. Creation draws us to God. Many churches bring creation to the big screen in the sanctuary to add to the worship service. Teaming two of our most powerful senses, hearing and sight, is a great tool to lead us to worship.

Yet we don't need tools to worship God. We can worship him anywhere, at any time. All we need is the proper frame of mind. When our focus is on him, rather than on the things of the world (self, others, problems, aspirations), we begin our worship experience. And then when we realize our sufficiency is in God alone, true worship erupts. It's not about a "proper" style of music, it is about a proper mindset of joy.

> God's amazing creation causes my heart to stop and consider his vastness. He is worthy of my worship in song, in prayer, in meditation, in admiration. No one compares to him!

What marvelous beauty is around me each day. God's amazing creation causes my heart to stop and consider his vastness. He is worthy of my worship in song, in prayer, in meditation, in admiration. No one compares to him! Let's determine to encourage others to have this attitude: *I will sing to the Lord as long as I live: I will sing praise to my God while I have my being* (Psalm 104:33 NKJV). Don't wait for Sunday to worship God!

Serve It Forward in Songs of Joy

Consider ways to encourage others to sing their own songs of joy. Sharing our faith doesn't have to start with mourning the death of Christ caused by our sin; it can start with rejoicing over the empty cross—the resurrection. Allow the joy of the resurrection to be contagious and then go back and fill in the blanks. That's the perfect time to share the full reason for your faith. After you share the joy of the resurrection, *then* tell how you needed a Savior to pay the price for your sin so you could be reunited with God. Next, point to Jesus on the cross as a sacrificial substitute. Then circle back to the power of the resurrection—the reason for your joy. What would happen if you shared a gospel message that starts and ends with joy?

Here are some joy-filled verses from Psalms to make real with others.

- *Satisfy us each morning with your unfailing love, so we may sing for joy to the end of our lives.* (Psalm 90:14)
- *You thrill me, Lord, with all you have done for me! I sing for joy because of what you have done.* (Psalm 92:4)
- *Worship the Lord with gladness. Come before him, singing with joy.* (Psalm 100:2)
- *Songs of joy and victory are sung in the camp of the godly. The strong right arm of the Lord has done glorious things!* (Psalm 118:15)
- *Everyone will share the story of your wonderful goodness; they will sing with joy about your righteousness.* (Psalm 145:7)

Your Grin-with-Joy Challenge

You've always been sort of cranky when it comes to hearing loud music. It never dawned on you that the listener might simply be captivated in a moment of worship. Now you want to experiment with your own personal worship styles using music. What can you do to fill up on joy as you fill up on music? What songs will you put on your playlist?

Chapter Ten

THE ENDURANCE OF *Joy*

The things we try to avoid and fight against—tribulation, suffering, and persecution—are the very things that produce abundant joy in us. "We are more than conquerors through him" "in all these things"; not in spite of them, but in the midst of them. A saint doesn't know the joy of the Lord in spite of tribulation, but *because* of it. Paul said, "I am exceedingly joyful in all our tribulation." —Oswald Chambers

Even in tremendous trials we can experience great joy because we abide in Christ. He equips us to endure hardship and to wait patiently for his good endings. We anticipate answered prayers while we continue to joyfully seek and serve him.

Grin with Joy

"I hate to always complain, but . . ." Lisa said, rehearsing for the tenth time the various trials in her life. I wanted to say, "Then STOP IT!" but I held back until Lisa took a breath. Then I jumped in to encourage her to change her focus if she didn't want to always complain.

She told me I didn't understand what it is like to have trials in my life, that no one had been through as much as she had been through in the past few years. I chose *not* to tell her about my own rocky life journey, but rather asked her to tell me some of the ways God had blessed her. She said there were many times, but that her negative circumstances were all she could think about.

Lisa lived like a defeated Christian. She found herself always complaining but didn't know how to stop. She rehearsed the same problems over and over in her mind (and to anyone who would listen). She *knew* others had gone through worse problems in their lives, but she *felt* as if no one had it any worse. She had developed a martyr's complex, and it was easier to wallow in her unhappiness than to work at getting out of the quicksand and onto solid ground.

> It was easier to wallow in unhappiness than to work at getting out of the quicksand and onto solid ground.

Lisa and I had run into each other at a meeting. I chose to stay to hear the speaker, while she ducked out early because of her complex life. Lisa could have benefited from the speech if she had stayed. She was sabotaging her own progress by not adding positive things to her life (like church, small group, accountability, inspirational music, a hobby, and most importantly, an intimate walk with Jesus). She wonders why she has few friends and doesn't realize people tire of hearing her sad saga.

We can learn from Lisa's story. Do we ever get so caught up in our own pitiful lives that we forget about the victory we have in Jesus? Do we choose to live joyless and hopeless lives without considering the God factor?

Whenever I feel tempted to sink into my own quicksand pity party, I think of Lisa. I don't want to be miserable like her, and more than that, I don't want to make others miserable to be around me. May we all choose joy!

How to Lose Weight in All the Right Places

"Weight loss tips" is the forty-second most searched-for-online keyword phrase as I write this, and it stays in the top five hundred most of the time. Why? Because almost all of us are concerned about our weight. Some worry about how they look and how their clothes fit. Others want to lose weight to improve health. Some lose weight to please others, some to please self. And sadly, most of us know more about how to lose weight than we actually *do* lose weight. I myself am a weight-loss veteran.

While I'm on a self-improvement kick that helps me physically, I also need to focus on losing a different kind of weight—the weight of self. I need to reduce the weight that hinders me from running the race God has put in front of me. He wants me to let go of any fault that rebels against his will and focus on the finish line. Even more challenging is the fact that God wants me to be patient when I endure the obstacles that get in the way of running my race.

> *Since we are surrounded by such a huge crowd of witnesses to the life of faith, let us strip off every weight that slows us down, especially the sin that so easily trips us up. And let us run with endurance the race God has set before us. We do this by keeping our eyes on Jesus, the champion who initiates and perfects our faith. Because of the joy awaiting him, he endured the cross, disregarding its shame. Now he is seated in the place of honor beside God's throne.* (Hebrews 12:1–2)

Here's my list of the top five *R*s for losing the weight of self so you can grow spiritually:

1. Remember your support system.
2. Remove any hindrance.
3. Repent of sin and watch for sin traps.
4. Run with patience—endure!
5. Remember the finish line, looking to Jesus.

I've never been much of a runner, and I especially never had the endurance to run long distances. But I sure like the idea of being a faith-race marathoner! As I run with patience, I hope to learn how to endure with joy. That might just be a better health plan than any diet or exercise routine.

> **It seems odd to think of the words *patience* and *waiting* in the same sentence as *joy*, but God makes it possible.**

Grow with Joy

The Bible teaches us to aspire to the virtue of endurance, and indicates tenacity enriches our joy. It seems odd to think of the words *patience* and *waiting* in the same sentence as *joy*, but God makes it possible.

> *You have given me greater joy than those who have abundant harvests of grain and new wine.* (Psalm 4:7)

We aren't always blessed with good times. Often life is about feast or famine. Feast tastes a lot better than famine; that is certainly true. But there's something about God's joy that is even sweeter during tough times. The psalmist explains it this way: God had given him such joy that it was greater (better, superior, larger, bigger) than the joy experienced by those who have an abundance of blessings.

> *Our hearts ache, but we always have joy. We are poor, but we give spiritual riches to others. We own nothing, and yet we have everything.* (2 Corinthians 6:10)

Paul acknowledged to the Corinthians that his life wasn't always happy but that he always had joy. Even when our hearts ache, we can have joy. Always—forever, for all time, for eternity, until the end of time, forever and a day! Paul explained how to have never-ending joy: we can be joyful as we serve it forward with faith mentoring. It's like we own it all, even when we own nothing at all.

> *You received the message with joy from the Holy Spirit in spite of the severe suffering it brought you. In this way, you imitated both us and the Lord.* (1 Thessalonians 1:6)

When Paul wrote this passage to the Thessalonians, he acknowledged their suffering—other versions even refer to it as persecution. They were also known for being faithful followers of the Lord. They desired to be mentored and through that process, they welcomed Paul's message with joy—a joy that came from the Holy Spirit. Has there ever been a time when you experienced unexplainable joy despite enduring a trial?

If you trace the source back, perhaps you too will find it started as you received God's Word. Then it grew as you became more aware of God's presence in your life through the Holy Spirit.

> *Dear brothers and sisters, when troubles of any kind come your way, consider it an opportunity for great joy.* (James 1:2)

THE ENDURANCE OF JOY

When troubles come your way, what is your first tendency? To call a friend and vent? To sigh, whine or cry? To rant with rage? What if you tried to consider it an opportunity to experience great joy? Not just an opportunity for others to observe you reflecting the joy of the Lord, but an opportunity for you to experience such a superhuman emotion, considering the circumstances. This kind of joy can't be worked up or summoned by your own strength and abilities—it has to start with emptying you of *you* and getting filled up with God's presence. Then he is free to operate in and through you. At that point, the trouble seems less traumatic and the joy is overwhelmingly magnificent. Such great joy, not merely despite the circumstances, but *because* of them.

> *Be truly glad. There is wonderful joy ahead, even though you have to endure many trials for a little while.* (1 Peter 1:6)

Enduring trials and experiencing joy seem to go together. What does it mean to be *truly glad*? What other sorts of gladness might there be?

Knowing there is wonderful joy ahead assists a sad or mad person in being truly glad. Recognizing there are trials to endure first is more tolerable when we realize any sort of trouble is temporary.

What a welcome relief the word *temporary* is. My Grandma Mary used to remind herself, "This too shall pass." I tried saying that when I had my own trials, but sometimes the burdens still seemed heavy. Then I converted the deep concept into a plainer statement (I'm a simple girl who needs simple concepts). Now I use self-talk like "It's only temporary." Lightbulb moment: I can endure this because it's not going to last forever. What is in my future is so incredible, I can be truly glad—even before it gets here!

> **I can endure this because it's not going to last forever. What is in my future is so incredible, I can be truly glad—even before it gets here!**

> *Instead, be very glad—for these trials make you partners with Christ in his suffering, so that you will have the wonderful joy of seeing his glory when it is revealed to all the world.* (1 Peter 4:13)

What a mind-blowing principle, to know that when we suffer, we enter into the fellowship of Christ's suffering. It's one of those join-the-club moments. How can we be *very glad* when we have trials? By focusing on the wonderful joy of anticipating the glory to come. (I know this for a certainty because I peeked and read the back of the book!)

The word *instead* indicates that what follows is something that doesn't come naturally to us without God's strength. To be glad during trials—that's not a human trait, but a godly one. It's not that we rejoice in the actual trial, but we're glad God never changes even when circumstances change. We get to abide in him (oh, the blessing of that thought!), rather than sink into our own problems. We are Christ's partners and are assured of seeing his glory.

> *Yet I will rejoice in the LORD! I will be joyful in the God of my salvation!* (Habakkuk 3:18)

The word *yet* shows us that no matter how many negatives engulf our list of life experiences (the trials, the challenges, the suffering), we can rejoice in the Lord. *I will rejoice* is a statement of determination. It's an image of digging our heels in, saying "This is where I stand!" Why is Habakkuk able to be joyful?

Habakkuk's joy was in the God of his salvation. He received contentment, peace, and gladness from the one who rescued him. If we look at what God provides us through salvation, we too can rejoice.

Go with Joy

Take action this week by swapping the typical emotions of suffering for the atypical emotion of joy. Look up the lyrics to "Trading My Sorrows" by songwriter Darrell Evans. A perfect resolution!

Action Steps to Joy

Read Hebrews 10:32–26 in your Bible and choose some of the following steps from that passage to begin to act on now.

1. **Reflect on your life as a new believer.** *Think back on those early days when you first learned about Christ* (Hebrews 10:32).
2. **Determine to stay faithful even if it results in painful trials and challenges.** *Remember how you remained faithful even though it meant terrible suffering* (Hebrews 10:32).
3. **Endure hardship without giving up, even when it hurts your reputation.** *Sometimes you were exposed to public ridicule and were beaten* (Hebrews 10:33).
4. **Help others with similar struggles.** *And sometimes you helped others who were suffering the same things* (Hebrews 10:33).
5. **Accept suffering and loss with joy.** *You suffered along with those who were thrown into jail, and when all you owned was taken from you, you accepted it with joy* (Hebrews 10:34).
6. **Bear up cheerfully by keeping your hope in what is yet to come.** *You knew there were better things waiting for you that will last forever* (Hebrews 10:34).
7. **Cling to your fearless confidence in God.** *So do not throw away this confident trust in the Lord* (Hebrews 10:35).
8. **Keep the prize in mind when you feel like quitting.** *Remember the great reward it brings you!* (Hebrews 10:35).
9. **Endure with patience so you continue to accomplish God's will.** *Patient endurance is what you need now, so that you will continue to do God's will* (Hebrews 10:36).
10. **Obey joyfully, anticipating a good outcome.** *Then you will receive all that he has promised* (Hebrews 10:36).

What does the word *endure* mean to you?

What has been the most difficult trial for you to endure?

How does patience influence your ability to experience joy?

Share a time when you experienced a supernatural joy during a terrible time in your life.

Name someone in whom you've observed joy even during trials. What can we learn from him or her?

Give with Joy

God's Word helps us offer hope to those who are waiting for things to get better. Can you think of someone growing weary in the pursuit of joy?

Serve It Forward to Help Another Endure with Joy

Consider paraphrasing a passage of Scripture to give to someone suffering through a terrible trial. Ask God to show you whom to encourage, and which passage he wants you to personalize for them. I recently used the principles found in the first chapter of Colossians to encourage a pastor's wife going through an overwhelming challenge.

Letter to a Friend
Inspired by Colossians 1

This letter is from Kathy, chosen by the will of God to be a Christ follower, and a sister-friend to [Name Here]—also a called-out believer.

May God our Joy-Bearer give you grace and peace.

I pray for you often, thanking God for you. Your love for him and for others is well-known by any who know you—a testimony of your faithfulness. Even when you struggle with day-to-day issues, he reminds you that you can have a confident hope of all he has reserved for you in heaven. Ever since you came to know him, you have been filled with anticipation and expectation of what is yet to come. It is harder for you to grasp how to deal with the here and now, but God has the answers for that as well.

This same good news that came to you when you first believed has the power to change others (and continue to change you). You can make a difference by being a living testimony of God's transformation, still at work in you. Even this current struggle can be one more beautiful testimony of God's wonderful grace. His story of redemption and transformation, told through you—the pages of your book, the days and years of your life.

God brings others into our lives to help us when we don't know where to turn. They are God's faithful servants to minister to you (and to me). Just as you have been a faithful servant—even when you don't feel like it—even when you fall short. Still, that love remains in you, just as the Holy Spirit remains in you.

Because of this great love I have for you and for God, I have not stopped praying for you. I continue to ask God to give you complete knowledge of his will and to give you spiritual wisdom and understanding. This special endowment of grace will continue to be enough to help you know the way he wants you to live so that you will always have the opportunity to honor and please the Lord, that your life will produce every kind of good fruit. All the while, you will grow as you learn to know God better and better.

I'm also praying you will be strengthened with his glorious power so you will have all the endurance and patience you need. May you be filled with joy, always thanking the Father. He has enabled you and will continue to equip you as you share in the inheritance that belongs to his people, who live in the light.

He has rescued us from the kingdom of darkness and transferred us into the kingdom of his dear Son, who purchased our freedom and forgave our sins. Never forget, he continues to save those he has rescued from the darkness of the deep—we remain his *projects* until the day he perfects us—the day we are brought to his side. The Creator of everything has all power to complete this work he has started in you.

God is close to you, even when you feel far away from him, feeling distant because of your weaknesses and temptations, including the struggles of your thoughts and actions. He continues to reconcile you to himself through the death of Christ. Because you have put on Christ in your life, the heavenly Father sees Christ's virtue and holiness rather than the self- and Satan-induced flaws that initially separated you from him. He sees the very perfection of Jesus, holy and blameless, as if you stand before him without a single fault.

But you must continue to believe this truth and stand firmly in it. Don't drift away from the assurance you received when you first heard and received the good news.

God's secrets and mysteries are revealed to God's people through the Holy Spirit and through his Word because God wants us to know that the riches and glory of Christ are available to us—*even* us. And this is the secret: Christ lives in you. This gives you assurance of sharing his glory.

So we continue to work out the ending of our story—this life we live in Christ. And because what we face is common to others, we have a story to which they relate. When we tell others about Christ, we can tell them what God is doing in our lives—the ending he is still writing in us. And we get to be a part, as flawed as we are, with the harvest of souls, delivered to our God. That's why we work and struggle so hard. It's worth it all. May we continue to depend on Christ's mighty power at work within us.

Your Grin-with-Joy Challenge

You just found out that the symptoms you thought were caused by a cold that won't go away isn't a cold at all. It's an autoimmune disease with no cure. First, you give in to the grief—the loss of the life you have known. But as you pray your burdens to the Lord, he embraces you and encourages you to seek joy as the best medicine for this trial. How can you possibly be joyful with this overwhelming diagnosis? What biblical promise do you cling to as these trials attempt to rob you of your joy?

Chapter Eleven

THE TEARS OF *Joy*

> We enjoy warmth because we have been cold. We appreciate light because we have been in darkness. By the same token, we can experience joy because we have known sadness. —DAVID WEATHERFORD

We experience joy even when weeping, in the midst of suffering and mourning, knowing the blessing of God's presence in our lives. God inspires rejoicing despite the grief. Only in him can we surrender our anguish and experience a joy that humanly doesn't make sense.

Grin with Joy

My mother-in-love, Lula Mae Willis, always joked about being born on Groundhog Day. My husband was also due on that date, but stubbornly waited until February 8 to arrive. This way, his mom got a day all to herself.

Mom Willis was one of my role models. I'll never attain to her skills as a homemaker and frugal shopper, but she gave me her heart for helping tween and teen girls. She attentively listened to them—not just hearing them but enjoying their company, and she always had two or three "adopted" well after her own girls left home. She sang hymns with gusto and listened intently to sermons. She was uncomfortable in the water, especially before moving to a home that had its own pool, and it was a real act of faith when she was baptized by immersion. She always said as long as her feet could touch the bottom and her hair didn't get wet, she could deal with being in the water—obviously immersion broke one of those rules! She had a giving heart and loved seeing and meeting needs, often sensing someone was hurting when no one else noticed.

In 1994, Mom Willis found out she had breast cancer. Three years later the cancer had spread, and she knew deep down this would be her last year to live. Eventually there was nothing more medical science could provide her in the way of hope, but she was not hopeless. Her hope remained in Jesus Christ until her last breath.

My mother-in-love had a tremendous faith. Her relationship with God was evident as she endured the effects of the cancer, the chemo, and the radiation. She knew she wasn't suffering alone—God was with her every step of the way. Even on days when she couldn't read her Bible, she had someone else read it to her. She shed tears during her cancer journey, but she always clung to hope that lasted well beyond what was ahead for her time on earth.

> When you visit the tear shed and the trials of life knock you off your feet, trust in God to continually baptize you with the waterfalls of peace and joy.

I learned a lot from Mom Willis about trusting God no matter what. When she whispered good-bye to this life it wasn't because she lost her fight with cancer, it was because God called her to her real home—with him. (There is no defeat in death, merely graduation!) Then it was our turn to cry buckets of tears—crying out in sorrow, yes—but also rejoicing because of our love for her. We celebrated a life well spent.

When you visit the tear shed and the trials of life knock you off your feet, trust in God to continually baptize you with the waterfalls of peace and joy. When you're heartsick with the sorrows of this life, determine to praise him anyway—even if through the tears. Often those honest moments with God are the times we most realize his abiding presence in our lives.

> *There I will go to the altar of God, to God—the source of all my joy. I will praise you with my harp, O God, my God! Why am I discouraged? Why is my heart so sad? I will put my hope in God! I will praise him again—my Savior and my God!* (Psalm 43:4–5)

Lumpy-Throat Syndrome

Three events in one week elicited a lump in my throat. You know the sensation I'm talking about—when it seems tears are imminent.

First, I found a lump in my throat during my final mental preparations to sing "The National Anthem" for our area Relay for Life event. I looked out into the audience and discovered a turban decorating a baldheaded woman. Suddenly I flashed back to the memory of my mother-in-love wearing her own turban. It hit me like a ton of bricks why the Relay for Life was so important. What a great cause! Realizing these cancer survivors and family members sacrificed so much to participate touched me in a deep spot down in my heart. Have you ever tried to prepare to sing for an event with a lump in your throat?

> Whether you care for a cause, a country, or someone's wellbeing, you act out the heart of Christ.

Then the color guard marched to the stand in full regalia. The uniforms and the flag tugged at my heart. Their presentation of our stars and stripes reminded me of everything our country has given up over the years. The red reminded me of the blood shed; the blue, the loyalty of the military; and the white, that our country has stood for all that is right in this world. Thinking of what our country has gone through in recent years only intensified the lump in my throat. Have you ever tried to sing our national anthem with a lump in your throat?

The lumpy throat returned on Mother's Day. I spoke at church to a class of junior high girls and announced I would be their new teacher. During the worship service, the kids were encouraged to sit with their mothers and to present them with a gift provided by the church in appreciation for all they do. Knowing I am childless, one of my new students asked if she could sit by me. And when the gift presentations were made, she retrieved one for me. Who wouldn't get a lump in her throat from such a loving act of kindness? Ashleigh reminded me that you don't have to be a biological mother to nurture others on their life journeys.

I'm sure each of you has had this lumpy-throat syndrome at some point in your lives. My conclusion is that the lump is merely a symptom of something bigger. It means we care. A person who does not truly care does not truly live.

Whether you care for a cause, a country, or someone's wellbeing, you act out the heart of Christ. Care enough to share your life in Christ with others. What a precious source of joy!

Grow with Joy

We've all heard the term *tears of joy*. Let's see what the Bible tells us about this topic.

Weeping with joy, he embraced Benjamin, and Benjamin did the same. (Genesis 45:14)

Tears don't always indicate grief—sometimes they are shed during times of intense joy. Joseph was overcome with emotion as he hugged his dear brother Benjamin—reunited after a long separation. If you haven't cried lately, it doesn't necessarily mean life's been good—it could mean you haven't experienced a God-sized joy moment.

The joyful shouting and weeping mingled together in a loud noise that could be heard far in the distance. (Ezra 3:13)

Oftentimes, worship and celebration involve weeping as well as raising our voices in praise. In Jewish culture, weeping didn't mean a few tears leaking out of the corners of the eyes. No, weeping almost always involved what a Texan might call a caterwauling. Great drops of tears, accompanied by a high-volume scene to match the mournful or celebratory event. No wonder this passage describes the occasion as such a loud noise it could be heard a long distance away!

Those who plant in tears will harvest with shouts of joy. (Psalm 126:5)

How is it possible that something can start out in tears and end in joy? Often, the more our hearts are invested in a situation, the more grateful we are when God brings about a positive outcome.

He [Mordecai] told them to celebrate these days with feasting and gladness and by giving gifts of food to each other and presents to the poor. This would commemorate a time when the Jews gained relief from their enemies, when their sorrow was turned into gladness and their mourning into joy. (Esther 9:22)

THE TEARS OF JOY

The book of Esther shows the contrast of sorrow and gladness. What comfort is it to you to know your mourning can be turned to joy? Is this cause for a celebration?

Tears of joy will stream down their faces, and I will lead them home with great care.
They will walk beside quiet streams and on smooth paths where they will not stumble.
For I am Israel's father, and Ephraim is my oldest child. (Jeremiah 31:9)

While this passage is prophetic for the nation of Israel, it's interesting to note the action predicted to come. Can you imagine, after such a long journey, seeing your hope fulfilled? How special it would be to have such a gentle escort home, *with great care*. That makes me want to cry tears of joy simply thinking of it now.

I tell you the truth, you will weep and mourn over what is going to happen to me, but the world will rejoice. You will grieve, but your grief will suddenly turn to wonderful joy. (John 16:20)

Jesus warned the disciples of what was to come with his death, burial, and resurrection. Only they had to live it out to really believe it. I rejoice to know that weeping, mourning, and grieving can turn to such wonderful joy. Are there any troubles that aren't temporary, in the scope of things? Knowing this can bring such hope—such joy!

It will be like a woman suffering the pains of labor. When her child is born, her anguish gives way to joy because she has brought a new baby into the world. (John 16:21)

Labor pains are called *pains* for a reason! But the first time a mother lays eyes on her child, all tears are wiped away and in place of the moans are great bursts of joy. In this passage in John 16, Jesus is preparing his disciples for his death and resurrection.

So you have sorrow now, but I will see you again; then you will rejoice, and no one can rob you of that joy. (John 16:22)

Jesus continued to instruct the disciples about his death and resurrection. He assured them they would see each other again. Knowing we will see Jesus one day is certainly a cause for rejoicing. This verse says, *no one can rob you of that joy.* No matter what awful circumstance or situation you endure, no matter the tears you cry, nothing can take away the joy of knowing someday you will be united with Jesus, your Savior.

> **No matter what awful circumstance or situation you endure, no matter the tears you cry, nothing can take away the joy of knowing someday you will be united with Jesus, your Savior.**

The young women will dance for joy, and the men—old and young—will join in the celebration. I will turn their mourning into joy. I will comfort them and exchange their sorrow for rejoicing. (Jeremiah 31:13)

Children without a care in the world dance for joy, completely uninhibited, when they hear music or rhythm. When we don't have the cares of this world weighing us down, we feel light enough we could dance—and perhaps we do. God desires to turn our mourning into joy. Not happiness at our situation, but joy because of our permanent, eternal relationship with the Father.

I have given rest to the weary and joy to the sorrowing. (Jeremiah 31:25)

Toddlers often fight naps, and the more tired they get, the easier it is for them to cry. When we need rest in our lives, even as grown-ups, our weariness feels like sorrow. God desires to give us a rest that brings great joy. And thankfully, we don't have to wait until heaven to receive this great blessing. His rest and his joy can be for us today.

Go with Joy

Would you consider keeping a journal of all the times you cried? To some, it's beneficial for healing, but for others it's merely a cause to wallow longer in self-pity. There used to be door-to-door salesmen who hawked their encyclopedia sets for sale. It came with multiple volumes of important facts. Would your tear journals take up a similar number of volumes? Use your imagination. How many books would it take if you recorded each time your heart hurt to the point of tears?

THE TEARS OF JOY

Well, even if we don't keep track of our crying jags, God stores up a record of our tears. *You keep track of all my sorrows. You have collected all my tears in your bottle. You have recorded each one in your book* (Psalm 56:8). The Message paraphrase of the Bible words it this way: *You've kept track of my every toss and turn through the sleepless nights, each tear entered in your ledger, each ache written in your book.*

Could the saltwater drops that leak from our eyes communicate in a special way to our heavenly Father or represent something of vital importance to him? Why does he save a reminder of our sorrow? Why do you think God wants to store up our tears?

The Lord watches over us with such gentle care and concern that our tears matter to him. What loving-kindness!

Action Steps to Joy

Our Father not only recognizes the cries of his children, but he hurts when we hurt. And he wants to soothe us—so much so that he sent us a Comforter. The Holy Spirit abides in us with a gift of peace—a source of joy. Rest assured; our tears are precious to the Lord.

> The Lord watches over us with such gentle care and concern that our tears matter to him. What loving-kindness!

1. **Recognize that God cares for you—He pays attention when you cry.** *Go back to Hezekiah and tell him, "This is what the L*ORD*, the God of your ancestor David, says: I have heard your prayer and seen your tears"* (Isaiah 38:5).
2. **Call out to God for help and wait for him to rescue you.** *The L*ORD *hears his people when they call to him for help. He rescues them from all their troubles. The L*ORD *is close to the brokenhearted; he rescues those whose spirits are crushed. The righteous person faces many troubles, but the L*ORD *comes to the rescue each time* (Psalm 34:17–19).

3. **Pour out your troubles to the Lord.** *My friends scorn me, but I pour out my tears to God* (Job 16:20).

4. **Remind yourself that in the end, God will wipe away all tears from our eyes.** *He will wipe every tear from their eyes, and there will be no more death or sorrow or crying or pain. All these things are gone forever* (Revelation 21:4).

5. **Burn your burden into ashes.** When times get tough, write down the situation on a piece of paper, then burn the paper into ashes. Put the cooled ashes in a resealable bag to remind you that just as that piece of paper was temporary, your situation is temporary too. It is a symbol that someday God will take the ashes of your awful scenario and exchange them for something so beautiful you can't even envision it. Attach this verse to the sack of ashes as a reminder: *To all who mourn in Israel, he will give a crown of beauty for ashes, a joyous blessing instead of mourning, festive praise instead of despair. In their righteousness, they will be like great oaks that the* L*ord* *has planted for his own glory* (Isaiah 61:3).

Think of a momentous time you cried tears of joy. What was the experience like for you?

Remember a time when you cried mournful tears to the point of caterwauling. What prompted such a drastic response? Did you find comfort or did the sorrow linger?

What comfort is it to know that God cares about your tears and longs to exchange your sorrow for joy?

Give with Joy

Earlier in this chapter I mentioned how my mother-in-love valiantly fought cancer. Despite her brave exterior, she struggled with crying spells. Uncontrollable tears spilled from her eyes with no notice. She hated the tears; she'd been taught tears represent weakness. Mom Willis wanted to be strong and fierce in her faith, not weak.

One day I found the verse I mentioned in *Go with Joy*. Psalm 56:8. It seemed to be in the Bible just for Mom Willis. I wrote out the verse on a slip of paper and gave it to her in a card.

I was with Mom Willis at the very end of her earthly life. Even as her body took its last grueling breath, one single tear slipped down her cheek. But this time, her eyes focused on the very source of her joy, and her lips turned upward, revealing a calm assurance, along with those beautiful dimples. Her tears of suffering had turned to tears of joy.

> Her eyes focused on the very source of her joy, and her lips turned upward, revealing a calm assurance. Her tears of suffering had turned to tears of joy.

When we went through her belongings, I found the slip of paper with my handwriting as a bookmark in her Bible, highlighting Psalm 56:8. What a comfort that verse first provided her, and there it was, to comfort me in my time of sorrow as well: *You keep track of all my sorrows. You have collected all my tears in your bottle. You have recorded each one in your book.*

Serve It Forward to Help Turn Tears to Joy

Is there someone you know going through a tough time? If the situation is appropriate, consider sharing Psalm 56:8 with your friend. Write it out in a special encouragement card. Let this person know you are praying for her. Reassure her of how special she is to God—and to you. In this way, you will be spreading God's joy by assuring your friend that her suffering is only temporary.

Your Grin-with-Joy Challenge

You don't know why, but it's another day of crying. You just can't stop. You think you have control over the tears, but then a sad commercial comes on TV and you weep again. You feel so alone in your tears. How can you remind yourself that God is near and he cares, as you go through this tearful time? Does focusing on his presence in your life lead to renewed joy despite the tears?

Chapter Twelve

THE BENEFITS OF *Joy*

When you wish someone joy, you wish them peace, love, prosperity, happiness . . . all the good things. —Maya Angelou

The Lord gives us blessings as we seek him. We embrace his good gifts and rejoice with thanksgiving. We delight in the results of placing our lives in his hands. It is our joy to see his amazing works through us and to us on this faith journey.

Grin with Joy

Thanks*living*. No, it's not a typo! Rather than celebrating Thanksgiving once a year, let's show our gratitude daily by *thanksliving*—counting our many blessings. As the old song goes, do we really name them one by one? If I were to journal my blessings, I could not find a book large enough to contain the list.

God consistently desires to give us good gifts. *Whatever is good and perfect is a gift coming down to us from God our Father, who created all the lights in the heavens. He never changes or casts a shifting shadow* (James 1:17).

Our Lord enjoys our praises. Psalm 92:1 says, *It is good to give thanks to the Lord. God inhabits praise* (Psalm 22:3 KJV), meaning he is in the midst of praise. We risk taking God for granted in the absence of praise and thankfulness. Shakespeare said, "How sharper than a serpent's tooth is an ungrateful child." The serpent in this quote has often been compared to the devil and the ungrateful child to God's children who neglect to thank and praise their heavenly Father.

> We risk taking God for granted in the absence of praise and thankfulness.

Sadly, we have raised American children to develop a sense of entitlement. Many believe they have a right to receive certain things regardless of whether they act responsibly or show appreciation. Perhaps we, as God's children, are also guilty of feeling entitled to his blessings. Thankfully, he loves us despite our shortcomings. When we realize the good in life is because of who he is, rather than who we are, we can come to him just as we are and thank him for the many evidences of his loving-kindness in our lives.

Thanks*living* is a whole new way to give thanks!

Too Much!

It's just too much! Too much pain, too much suffering, too much confusion. Between several of my friends, there is entirely too much bad stuff going on. How does God expect us to cope when trials are so severe? One of my closest friends died of cancer at age 50, and others have faced serious diagnoses. Another friend has had such a terrible time at work that she says she is rehearsing her "I quit" speech, just in case she is pushed to her breaking point. And yet another friend is so overwhelmed by all the demands in her life that she says she can't take one more thing.

Isn't it odd that we tell God when things get to be too much—as in too much negative—but we never tell him when we're blown away because things are *too good?* With our soured perspectives, do we ever even have the perspective that God is blessing us too much? Do we ever ask him to take some blessings back because we can't handle it? I doubt it!

I started keeping a gratitude list a few years ago. It's a great exercise of discipline when my outlook stinks. At least twice a week, I list some blessings for which I am grateful. I doubt God gets tired of hearing us praise him for his goodness and for the beauty of his creation. Never does he say "too much."

What are you thankful for today? List your blessings.

I make it a point not to be thankful merely for the big things. By being grateful for the small things, I develop a thankful attitude no matter what the big bad wolf has brought my way. A sample gratitude list from my journal:

I'm grateful for:

- Medical treatments that make me feel so much better.
- A conversation with a friend who *gets it.*
- A milder summer than last year.
- More opportunities for work than I can take on.
- Pepsi Zero Sugar before noon!

See how throwing a simple item in your gratitude list makes you smile? Why not rehearse your gratitude to the Lord? Gratitude lists magnify the positive and diminish the negative in my life. May the same be true for you. *Let us come to him with thanksgiving. Let us sing psalms of praise to him* (Psalm 95:2).

> God gives every believer plenty of perks when it comes to this joy-thing.

Grow with Joy

There's a great deal the Bible says and doesn't say about the benefits of joy. It's important not to claim a Bible promise not meant for us. But God gives every believer plenty of perks when it comes to this joy-thing.

You will enjoy the fruit of your labor. How joyful and prosperous you will be! (Psalm 128:2)

There's a lot of incorrect doctrine on the subject of prosperity, so I want to caution us not to pull a Scripture verse out of context and try to apply it as a promise to our own situation. But we can look at this psalm and learn some concepts. When we labor, we don't have to begrudge our work; we can enjoy the end results. When was the last time you took joy in your work—or even considered it a blessing?

Yes, joyful are those who live like this! Joyful indeed are those whose God is the Lord. (Psalm 144:15)

Prior to this verse in Psalm 144, the psalmist lists ways those whom God rescues and prospers are blessed. Living like a rescued follower of God brings joy. Making God Lord, meaning that he leads our lives, is another ingredient in receiving joy. The benefits of serving God are countless and make us joyful—full of joy.

With joy you will drink deeply from the fountain of salvation! (Isaiah 12:3)

When you think of salvation being a fountain, isn't it interesting to imagine taking a deep sip and tasting joy? My granny had a well on her property. We'd send down the metal bucket into that deep, dark hole in the earth and bring up the coldest, purest-tasting water. We'd haul the pail into the house and place it on the counter, along with the matching dipper. Any time we were thirsty, we didn't need a glass; we could just ladle up this refreshing goodness. Jesus said if we partook of him we'd never thirst again, because he quenches our spiritual thirst (John 4:14). That's reason for joy!

But those who die in the Lord will live; their bodies will rise again! Those who sleep in the earth will rise up and sing for joy! For your life-giving light will fall like dew on your people in the place of the dead! (Isaiah 26:19)

Our joy doesn't stop when we breathe our last breath. No—after believers go to be with the Lord, the joy they experience certainly must be a high-def version of the joy we know on earth. If we feel like singing now, with all the turbulence of this life, just think how much we'll feel like singing for joy when we meet God face to face.

Another special part of this verse is thinking about his *life-giving light*. Most plants need light to keep them alive and to grow. God's light is necessary to give us life—new life in him. I think of a prisoner who has been set free after new DNA evidence comes in declaring him innocent. Free to leave the prison, he says the light that shines when he first steps on free soil is the brightest light ever to hit his eyes. When God frees us, we experience that sort of light, shining on us and through us. We appreciate the new life so much more after being released from the captivity of our old sin- and self-filled life.

> **Blessings tend to overshadow sorrows when we allow our focus to be on his joy. What good gifts has the Lord brought you today?**

> *They will come home and sing songs of joy on the heights of Jerusalem. They will be radiant because of the LORD's good gifts—the abundant crops of grain, new wine, and olive oil, and the healthy flocks and herds. Their life will be like a watered garden, and all their sorrows will be gone.* (Jeremiah 31:12)

When we recognize the good gifts that come from the Lord, we become radiant and we are moved to sing songs of joy. Blessings tend to overshadow sorrows when we allow our focus to be on his joy. What good gifts has the Lord brought you today?

Even on your worst day, there is always the comfort of some blessing God has given to you. Determine to find and focus on that blessing rather than on sorrow, not in a Pollyanna-like way—denying your trials, but in a step of faith, trusting him through it all.

> *For the L*ORD *your God is living among you. He is a mighty savior. He will take delight in you with gladness. With his love, he will calm all your fears. He will rejoice over you with joyful songs.* (Zephaniah 3:17)

God loves to bless us! List the benefits of our Lord mentioned in this verse.

Read over your list. You would think that the last sentence of this Scripture would say: "I will rejoice over the Lord with joyful songs." But no, it names another blessing—the Lord rejoices over *us*! Isn't that mind-blowing?

> *For the Kingdom of God is not a matter of what we eat or drink, but of living a life of goodness and peace and joy in the Holy Spirit.* (Romans 14:17)

I admit to being an epicurean when it comes to food. But the kingdom of God is more than the most scrumptious gourmet meal. It's about living a life of what?

How might goodness, peace, and joy go together in God's kingdom?

And why is the Holy Spirit vital to this life of goodness, peace, and joy?

Your love has given me much joy and comfort, my brother, for your kindness has often refreshed the hearts of God's people. (Philemon 1:7)

In his letter to Philemon, the apostle Paul requests restoration and freedom for a runaway slave, Onesimus, who had become a Christian. Paul reminds Philemon of the bond they share and thanks him for that love. Can you think of someone to whom you could write a similar note? Has someone given you much joy, comfort, and kindness, to the point that it has refreshed you as well as the hearts of many of God's people? Oh to be that kind of refreshment for someone!

Go with Joy

When you haven't plugged in to God's strength, do you notice you also have a deficit of joy? Strength and joy seem to go together like peanut butter and chocolate.

> *We also pray that you will be strengthened with all his glorious power so you will have all the endurance and patience you need. May you be filled with joy.* (Colossians 1:11)

Look what pumps up your God-given strength according to this verse:

- Praying for it (you pray for it and have others praying for it too).
- Making sure you are being filled up with *all* his glorious power.
- Receiving enough endurance and patience to supply your need.

Then the verse says, *May you be filled with joy.* Sure seems like having these actions in your life might lead to an increase of being filled with joy, doesn't it?

Action Steps to Joy

If you want to acquire the benefits of joy, don't wait for it to find you—instead determine to step out in faith to pursue it. Here are some ideas to get you started.

1. **Focus on your faith walk and tap in to your God-given strength.** *What joy for those whose strength comes from the* LORD, *who have set their minds on a pilgrimage to Jerusalem* (Psalm 84:5).

2. **Choose joy, even in conflict.** This is a tremendous benefit for Christ followers. No one is comfortable with conflict. But God's joy can give you peace. Read this example of two women in conflict and see what Paul suggests: *Now I appeal to Euodia and Syntyche. Please, because you belong to the Lord, settle your disagreement. And I ask you, my true partner, to help these two women, for they worked hard with me in telling others the Good News. They worked along with Clement and the rest of my co-workers, whose names are written in the Book of Life. Always be full of joy in the Lord. I say it again—rejoice! Let everyone see that you are considerate in all you do. Remember, the Lord is coming soon* (Philippians 4:2–5).

3. **Consider the joy experienced when the lost is found.** We are the sheep, and Christ is our shepherd. He rejoices when he finds us, and the angels in heaven rejoice. But certainly the found are joy-filled too! *If a man has a hundred sheep and one of them gets lost, what*

THE BENEFITS OF JOY

will he do? Won't he leave the ninety-nine others in the wilderness and go to search for the one that is lost until he finds it? And when he has found it, he will joyfully carry it home on his shoulders. When he arrives, he will call together his friends and neighbors, saying, "Rejoice with me because I have found my lost sheep." In the same way, there is more joy in heaven over one lost sinner who repents and returns to God than over ninety-nine others who are righteous and haven't strayed away! (Luke 15:4–7).

4. **Yield anything causing you to be disobedient to God.** Add in more trust and it will be easier to follow his lead. *The commandments of the LORD are right, bringing joy to the heart. The commands of the LORD are clear, giving insight for living* (Psalm 19:8).

5. **Permit the Holy Spirit to flow as joy through you.** Joy is a fruit of the Spirit. This means we don't have to work it up, we merely have to allow him to function by not restricting his work in and through us. *But the Holy Spirit produces this kind of fruit in our lives: love, joy, peace, patience, kindness, goodness, faithfulness, gentleness, and self-control. There is no law against these things!* (Galatians 5:22–23).

> Joy is a fruit of the Spirit. This means we don't have to work it up, we merely have to allow him to function by not restricting his work in and through us.

How can you have more strength from the Lord?

What one thing do you need to do differently to set your mind on your faith walk?

Go back to the *Grow with Joy* section of this chapter and underline or highlight every benefit of joy. Pick which one of these you need more of in your life.

Give with Joy

When I strolled through the Butterfly House and Gardens in Paris, Texas, the experience left me refreshed and relaxed. There's just something about nature—the greenery, the flowers, the scent of a recent rain that overrides any stress and burden. The workers strive hard to keep up with the gardening. One interesting point is that adults on probation work some of their community service hours at the gardens. Studies have found that gardening can change the lives of criminals for the better. No one can be involved with God's green earth and not be touched by his hand of blessing. Any time a person witnesses the plant breaking through the seed, the bud opening into a beautiful flower, or a butterfly emerging from the chrysalis, they are changed.

> One of the best places to talk with our Lord is in the quiet outdoor sanctuary of his creation.

God provided a garden like no other when he planted Adam and Eve smack-dab in the middle of the garden of Eden. They had no worries and only pleasant work to do. They were fed from the fruit of the garden, and they enjoyed walks through the garden with their Lord. I believe God surrounded the first of humankind with nature on purpose—we were designed to get pleasure from being in the garden, not fed merely physically, but also spiritually, emotionally, and mentally. One of the best places to talk with our Lord is in the quiet outdoor sanctuary of his creation.

When was the last time you took a time-out to breathe deeply and see clearly?

If you are like me, you allow your schedule to get too busy and your pace too hurried to really see the beauty around you. Use all five senses to soak in the Lord's handiwork. Smell the aromatic plants and taste the flavors of their fruit. Allow your eyes to witness their beauty. Tune your ears to hear the birdsongs and the whispering winds. Taste, touch, hear, smell, and see that the Lord is good.

Our God is good anywhere and everywhere. But oh, in the garden life is extra good! God knew what he was doing when he created the earth and all its goodness, for his good pleasure and for ours. Write out a prayer to thank him for this beauty.

The probationers who work in the butterfly garden aren't merely transformed because of their time gardening, but also because volunteers mentor them. In the same way, we can help others be changed by introducing them to more of God's blessings. What can you do to help someone else experience the transformational power of his creation—the power of his loving-kindness and blessing upon their lives?

Everything the Father has created is beautiful. May we drink up the air of his blessings, and like a chrysalis, may we be transformed by our Creator and Lord.

Serve It Forward to Help Others See the Benefits of Joy

As trials come into your life, it's easy to focus on the negative. Determine not to let that happen when you are in one of life's waiting rooms. Instead, look for the good things going on around you. Look for the way God inundates you with blessings. God often uses people to touch his hurting children. Sometimes it's our turn to be a blessing to others, so they might be encouraged in the Lord. Other times it's our turn to receive the blessing. Be aware of what you can do to serve it forward so others see the benefits of joy.

I've experienced firsthand what a blessing it is when others heed God's direction to take care of my needs. Without these Good Samaritans, where would I be? Where would any of us be without the caring aid of others? Unfortunately, sometimes it takes a trial to remind us how good it is to be in God's hands.

A movie a few years ago showed what it's like to do random acts of kindness. There was no spiritual application in the movie, but one could easily be drawn from it. It's not about "You scratch my back, I scratch yours." When we are blessed by someone, rather than reciprocating, it might be more meaningful to show kindness to a third party. We will find, while we are looking out for the needs of others, that God takes care of our own needs. It is a chain reaction of goodness.

> *If you love only those who love you, what reward is there for that?*
> *Even corrupt tax collectors do that much.* (Matthew 5:46)

> *Love your enemies! Do good to them. Lend to them without expecting to be repaid. Then your reward from heaven will be very great, and you will truly be acting as children of the Most High, for he is kind to those who are unthankful and wicked.* (Luke 6:35)

Take a risk this week. Be a blessing to someone in an unusual way. You will be surprised how good it feels! And while you are at it, count your own blessings. You will be amazed how many add up!

Your Grin-with-Joy Challenge

You hear the hymn "Count Your Blessings" and are reminded once again to be grateful. Then on the way home, Laura Story sings "Blessings" on the radio and your cheeks are washed with tears. You want to know the joy of finding blessings even in the bad times. You know it's a beautiful discipline that produces joy. You hear about other people who keep gratitude lists, but they have everything going for them. How can you possibly be thankful with what's going on in *your* life?

What does your gratitude list look like today as you seek joy? (And don't forget it's okay to list tiny little blessings if you can't find any big ones right now.)

Chapter Thirteen

THE ABUNDANCE OF *Joy*

Keep bubbling over with abundant joy, peace, and love. You may be the only well-watered oasis for someone going through a desert in their lives. —Caroline Naoroji

Just as we enjoy abundant life in Christ, we also delight in the abundance of his joy. It fills us and overflows from us. The supply of his joy never runs out. All creation bursts forth in joyful praise.

Grin with Joy

"I love your accent!" I told seven-year-old Jared.

He gave me a funny look. "What accident?"

I went on to explain that I hadn't said *accident* and gave him a basic definition for *accent*. Jared's mother said he had picked up his Southern drawl from his father. I found it quite special that Jared talked like his daddy.

I wonder if I talk like my heavenly Father? Can others identify me as one of his children because of my speech? Do I glorify and honor him with my words? The Bible explains that what proceeds out of our mouths is what dwells in our hearts (Matthew 15:18 KJV). I need to have the right heart condition to have the right words. When I have the heart of God, I will speak godly words. In moments of weakness, when my guard is down, my tongue can get me into trouble if I have not stored a godly spirit in my heart. This is no short order!

I'm sure Jared's father beams at his son when he hears Jared talk like him. Perhaps he's even said, "Like father, like son." First Samuel 13:14 calls David a man after God's own heart. It would be the best words I could ever hear if God said I'm a woman after his own heart.

A soft drink, when shaken, spills its contents. Similarly, a person shaken by the trials of life will reveal whatever is truly inside by what words come out. Will you bubble with excitement and overflow with joy, or will toxic words erupt from your heart?

It's never too late to get a heart transplant. God is always a willing donor.

Running on Empty

Have you ever been empty? Empty from dealing with your own issues (health, finances, pleasing God and others). Empty from dealing with others (heartache, death, disappointments). So empty that if you were a car, your fuel-warning indicator would be lit?

I hit that point recently. My physical stamina was nonexistent. My emotional stamina was drained from putting myself in others' shoes in order to minister to them. I kept filling my cup up with all the good things I need: rest, spiritual refreshment, me time, but I poured out my cup to deal with others faster than I could fill it up. Before I knew it, my inner being was dehydrated.

What do you do when this happens to you?

Just as when we I'm physically dehydrated, I have to put everything aside and hook up to an IV to be infused with all the things my inner spirit is missing. Take a break from "being all things to all people" and spend time nourishing my soul meditating on God's Word. Use an ice pack for body aches or take a long, hot bath. Allow time for my strength to build back up. And yes, have chocolate for a little pick-me-up!

O God, you are my God; I earnestly search for you. My soul thirsts for you; my whole body longs for you in this parched and weary land where there is no water. I have seen you in your sanctuary and gazed upon your power and glory. Your unfailing love is better than life itself; how I praise you! (Psalm 63:1–3)

It's always better to operate out of the abundance of our overflow when we give of ourselves to others than to give them the supply that keeps us functioning. Just like a fountain must have a continual supply of water coming in to compensate for the water going out, we must allow time for the Spirit to flow through us. Then our joy tank is full, and we won't be running on fumes. His life flow leads to joy.

Grow with Joy

Let the sea and everything in it shout his praise! Let the fields and their crops burst out with joy! (1 Chronicles 16:32)

Let the fields and their crops burst out with joy! Let the trees of the forest sing for joy. (Psalm 96:12)

*Sing for joy, O heavens! Rejoice, O earth! Burst into song, O mountains! For the L*ORD *has comforted his people and will have compassion on them in their suffering.* (Isaiah 49:13)

How does God's creation praise him? How does it express joy?

In the creation account found in the book of Genesis, we see God declaring it all *good*. He finds joy and pleasure in what he has created. And when we study the fascinating wonders of creation, we observe that everything made by God brings glory to him in some way.

> **When joy bursts, it means the object containing the joy is so full of what's inside that the joy breaks loose and overflows, bubbling over. This sort of joy is contagious.**

Let's focus on a key word found in each of these three verses: *burst*. Have you ever thought what it might mean to burst with joy? When I try on an outfit that fit me last year but is too snug now, I burst from the seams, and not in a good way! When we get too much rain, the levees sometimes burst. When we make popcorn the old-fashioned way, we can watch the fluffy treats burst from the kernels. When joy bursts, it means the object containing the joy is so full of what's inside that the joy breaks loose and overflows, bubbling over. This sort of joy is contagious and doesn't deplete the joy of the original joy giver.

> *I am overwhelmed with joy in the LORD my God! For he has dressed me with the clothing of salvation and draped me in a robe of righteousness. I am like a bridegroom in his wedding suit or a bride with her jewels.* (Isaiah 61:10)

Look at the reason for abundant joy here: salvation and righteousness, given freely to us by our Lord. Isaiah describes these gifts as ceremonial clothing or jewelry—the best of the best a man or woman might ever wear. The significance of our salvation, not to mention the magnitude of putting on Jesus' righteousness in place of our filthy rags of unrighteousness (Isaiah 64:6), is enough to overwhelm anyone with joy.

> *I have told you these things so that you will be filled with my joy. Yes, your joy will overflow!* (John 15:11)

I especially like it when I read words printed in red in the Gospels—the words of Christ. I imagine him speaking the words to the disciples while I'm there, eavesdropping. Some of the words were intended just for the actual hearer, and some of the words were meant for readers like me today. In your Bible, read John 15 to see what Jesus told his disciples so they could be filled to overflowing with his joy.

> *You haven't done this before. Ask, using my name, and you will receive, and you will have abundant joy.* (John 16:24)

THE ABUNDANCE OF JOY

Jesus talked to the disciples to prepare them for his crucifixion. He wanted them to know they could pray to the Father in his name, and they would receive what they asked for. The verse doesn't say, "Drop my name and you can have whatever you want, and God will put it on my tab." That's what some believers hope it means. *Using my name* means the request aligns with the mind and heart of Christ. Believers who pray this way will have abundant joy.

The verse doesn't say whether joy comes *because* we will receive what we asked for or whether joy is due to the prayer connection with the Father through the Son. Either way, this kind of prayer is a source for abundant (plentiful, copious, generous, bountiful) joy.

> *[God] never left them without evidence of himself and his goodness. For instance, he sends you rain and good crops and gives you food and joyful hearts.* (Acts 14:17)

I have a confession to make. I used to teach that only Christ followers could possess true joy, because the abiding of the Spirit is the source for joy. But here, as Paul spoke to unbelievers—the priest of the temple of Zeus and a crowd of Zeus worshippers—Paul declared to them the good news and said that God had always given them a reminder of his presence and his message. He never left them all alone, even though they chose not to follow him.

God shares his abundance with those outside his family as an opportunity for them to be drawn in. May they see the outpouring of his blessing.

> **God shares his abundance with those outside his family as an opportunity for them to be drawn in. May they see the outpouring of his blessing.**

> *I pray that God, the source of hope, will fill you completely with joy and peace because you trust in him. Then you will overflow with confident hope through the power of the Holy Spirit.* (Romans 15:13)

This passage shows what happens when we trust in God.

- He is _____ .
- He will _____.
- The power of his Spirit will_____.

They are being tested by many troubles, and they are very poor. But they are also filled with abundant joy, which has overflowed in rich generosity. (2 Corinthians 8:2)

The churches in Macedonia were sacrificially generous even though they lived in poverty. Paul mentioned their trials: they were *tested by many troubles*. But he highlighted the blessing—they were *filled with abundant joy*. Interesting the choice of the word *abundant*, because the next phrase uses a similar word to describe the Macedonians' giving—they *overflowed in rich generosity*.

> It is possible to be joyful even when we're going through tough times and money problems.

It is possible to be joyful even when we're going through tough times and money problems. It seems the more we give of ourselves and our resources, the more likely we will be filled all the way up (and over the top) with abundant joy.

Go with Joy

One fall season, my mom enjoyed picking up pecans so much from our yard that she picked up enough for her and her friends, and we also picked up enough for us. Still there were some left over, so we had a huge box of pecans sitting on our front porch. Then we noticed that *all* the pecans disappeared; only the empty box remained. Who would dare come up on our porch and steal our pecans out from under us but not take the box? The answer was right before our very eyes. Squirrels, of course! All winter long we noticed they seemed to be eating well, but we didn't realize we were the ones feeding them.

This is a trivial example of being robbed, but I do know of people who were robbed of their possessions, and they felt so violated. Sometimes the person who robbed them was someone they knew; other times, complete strangers invaded their personal space and stole their belongings. No matter the circumstances, being robbed attacks anyone's sense of security. Besides personal belongings, we are sometimes robbed of other things. Someone might even try to rob us of joy. But we have control of our joy, unlike when possessions are taken from us.

When joy is stolen, it isn't so the other party can possess our joy. No, when someone does something that causes us to quit being joyful, even though we say they robbed our joy, it's not as if they are now wearing our joy! They are usually as unhappy as we are when they have placed us in a negative situation.

THE ABUNDANCE OF JOY

Why is it we allow someone to steal our joy? Perhaps it's not even their motive to see us lose our peace and gladness. But when we allow circumstances or the actions of others to push our buttons, our joy departs.

The key is to realize this does not need to happen. We are the only ones who have access to our own control panels—no one else has our passwords. When we feel robbed of our joy, it is because we have allowed it to happen. Our source of joy is not in circumstances or other people, but in the peace of God, which passes all human understanding (Philippians 4:7).

> Were you fully relying on God, or did you allow circumstances (or people) to dictate your moods and emotions?

Think of a time you felt robbed of joy. Evaluate your attitude. Were you fully relying on God, or did you allow circumstances (or people) to dictate your moods and emotions? What can you do differently next time?

It's impossible to always be happy. Happiness is based on happenstance or circumstances, but situations change. Moods can change too if we don't allow our emotions to be controlled by someone who never changes—our heavenly Father. Our goal, rather, is to rejoice with joy that wells up deep within us and naturally overflows so we can share it with others.

Action Steps to Joy

In order to experience the abundance of joy, it's important to deal with any burdens weighing you down. Here are some specific steps you can take to de-stress.

1. **Don't be anxious.** Instead, vent your worries and frustrations to the Lord. *Don't worry about anything; instead, pray about everything. Tell God what you need, and thank him for all he has done* (Philippians 4:6).

2. **Deal with situations as they surface—don't let them accumulate.** *What this adds up to, then, is this: no more lies, no more pretense. Tell your neighbor the truth. In Christ's body we're all connected to each other, after all. When you lie to others, you end up lying to yourself. Go ahead and be angry. You do well to be angry—but don't use your anger as fuel for revenge. And don't stay angry. Don't go to bed angry. Don't give the Devil that kind of foothold in your life* (Ephesians 4:25–27 MSG).

3. **Control jealousy and anger in healthy ways.** Don't let others push your buttons. *People with understanding control their anger; a hot temper shows great foolishness. A peaceful heart leads to a healthy body; jealousy is like cancer in the bones* (Proverbs 14:29–30).

4. **Don't let someone else engage you in a guilt trip.** You don't need the frequent flyer miles that go along with that sort of journey! *Now there is no condemnation for those who belong to Christ Jesus* (Romans 8:1).

What is your weak spot when it comes to something or someone trying to steal your joy?

How can you shore up that weakness with God's reinforcements so you can stand against the tricks of the enemy?

What sort of mental or spiritual exercise might help you to experience the magnitude of God's overwhelming abundance of joy in your life?

What can you do to function with an abundance of joy, so you operate out of the overflow and avoid becoming depleted or burned out?

Give with Joy

One way to help others experience the abundance of joy is to add *kindness* to your to-do list. Offering kindness involves thoughtfulness, compassion, consideration, and helpfulness. Ask yourself, "What would I want others to do to help me if I were them?" Then set out to make it happen for them.

Serve It Forward to Help Others See the Abundance of Joy

Kindness can come to us in different forms. When we moved to a new community in Ohio, three young women (a nurse, a teacher, and a gymnast) helped us unpack our moving van. They not only displayed girl power but also grace. Yes, women who break a sweat and use their muscles can still be gracious. Why? Because their servant hearts glowed with the grace of kindness.

Other kindnesses greeted us to our new community. An anonymous farmer gave of his garden bounty. Freshly picked ears of corn waited at our doorstep. Our new church sent us flowers with a "Welcome to your new home" greeting. Another family shared from their overflowing pantry.

We've all been treated to the simple kindness of a good word, but we often overlook it. We get so caught up in the negativity of the day that we are blinded to the positive moments surrounding us. Sometimes, when I pillow my head at night, I ask myself, "What simple acts of kindness or words of grace did I share with others today?"

Being Christlike means not only mastering the large acts of godliness, but small kindnesses too. It is an accumulation of these simple acts that brings joy to the recipient as well as the giver. Let's set aside our human tendency to be self-absorbed and look for opportunities to spread joy.

> **Being Christlike means not only mastering the large acts of godliness, but small kindnesses too.**

Those who practice random acts of kindness say their own problems seem smaller. They become more grateful, and they walk with a spring in their steps. All from finding a way to brighten the day of another individual.

The first part of Ephesians 4:32 says, *Be kind to each other, tenderhearted.* How can we do that when we have so much frustration and bitterness? The remainder of the verse answers that question: *Forgiving one another, just as God through Christ has forgiven you.*

What if we declared tomorrow National Day of Kindness? Imagine the abundant joy that would occur!

Your Grin-with-Joy Challenge

You know the secret to grinning with joy is to allow God's joy to overflow from an abundant supply. But what does that look like in an ordinary day? How can you be joyful when you are late for choir rehearsal and you have a flat tire on the way? How can you allow joy to flow through you even then?

CONCLUSION

Serve It Forward with Joy

We wrap up this study focused on the Scriptures we need to go forth with his joy. We rejoice as we follow after truth and strengthen our trust and hope in him. And when we pursue God, *his* joy is also full.

The Lord is our source of joy. Having a heart of service is what primes the pump for joy to flow. See how the following verses indicate a serve-it-forward mentality regarding joy.

> *Whenever I pray, I make my requests for all of you with joy.* (Philippians 1:4)

Have you ever considered it joy to pray for others? Perhaps one reason our joy quotient is low is that we're not passionate enough to boldly beg God for answers on behalf of others who need his touch on their lives. As we pray and take on the heart of the Father concerning others, joy freely flows.

> *Therefore, my dear brothers and sisters, stay true to the Lord. I love you and long to see you, dear friends, for you are my joy and the crown I receive for my work.* (Philippians 4:1)

Do we find joy in mentoring others? As we share in the discipleship process, encouraging others to grow in the Lord, we will increase our joy.

> *After all, what gives us hope and joy, and what will be our proud reward and crown as we stand before our Lord Jesus when he returns? It is you!* (1 Thessalonians 2:19)

Our hope, our reward, our joy are all wrapped up in others.

> *Yes, you are our pride and joy.* (1 Thessalonians 2:20)

Those we mentor become like children in the Lord to us, our pride and joy.

> *How we thank God for you! Because of you we have great joy as we enter God's presence.* (1 Thessalonians 3:9)

We will have joy entering in the presence of God because we have not hoarded the goodness of God for ourselves—we have shared it with others. Let us be thankful for the opportunity to serve it forward.

> *I have much more to say to you, but I don't want to do it with paper and ink. For I hope to visit you soon and talk with you face to face. Then our joy will be complete.* (2 John 1:12)

Joy is completed when we are in fellowship with others. Don't isolate yourself. Make it a priority to be with others who love the Lord.

> *I could have no greater joy than to hear that my children are following the truth.* (3 John 1:4)

Seeing the results of mentoring has the ability to increase your joy more than anything else.

The final benediction as we close this study:

> *Now all glory to God, who is able to keep you from falling away and will bring you with great joy into his glorious presence without a single fault.* (Jude 1:24)

LEADER'S *Guide*

LEADER'S GUIDE

WEEK *One*

Together, read over the introduction and use it as a guide for setting up the study for future weeks.

Mixer

What personal, humorous, true-life observation can you add to the situations in "Just Grin with Joy, When…" in the introduction?

Discussion Questions

- When you think of the word *joy*, what comes to mind?
- Name a joyful woman you've met. How do you feel when you think of her? Tell us a little about her so we can learn from her life. How can you aspire to be like her?
- Can you think of someone in the Bible who exhibited joy? What can you learn from the way this person lived?
- What is your biggest challenge or struggle when it comes to reflecting joy to others?

Group Project

Discuss ideas for a group project, utilizing some of the *Go and Give with Joy* ideas from the book, or coming up with your own. How will you serve it forward with joy to benefit a designated group in some way? Adopt a project and spread the joy. Determine how this project schedule will work in to your seven weeks together.

Bible Verse

We ask God to give you complete knowledge of his will and to give you spiritual wisdom and understanding. Then the way you live will always honor and please the Lord, and your lives will produce every kind of good fruit. All the while, you will grow as you learn to know God better and better. We also pray that you will be strengthened with all his glorious power so you will have all the endurance and patience you need. May you be filled with joy, always thanking the Father. (Colossians 1: 9b–12a)

Grin Gal Pal Time

Draw names to pair up into Grin Gal Pals. You can keep the same Grin Gal Pal for the entire study or draw new pairs each week. After group time, attendees will meet in pairs and discuss these points:

- One prayer request for the coming week.
- One thought that surfaced from your study time (either a concept, a challenge, or another way God is at work).
- One goal for becoming more joyful in the week ahead.

Ask Grin Gal Pals to connect for prayer and encouragement with each other during this study. This can be done through text, messenger, voice message, email, lunch date or greeting card note. The method can be as varied as the group—it doesn't have to be the same for everyone.

Assignment

Read chapters 1 and 2 before the group's next meeting. Answer the questions as you go along to enhance your individual study and to prepare to participate in the group time.

Closing Prayer

Heavenly Father, thank you for bringing together this group to learn more about your joy. We realize any time we study about a virtue, that virtue will be challenged. So we pray each situation we face during this study will give us an opportunity to produce more joy in our own lives and also share joy with others. Shine the light on what you want us to discover about joy and help us apply it more in our everyday lives. Draw us nearer to you and to each other as we study your Word together. In the name of Jesus, and for his glory, amen.

WEEK *Two*

Mixer

- What story stands out to you the most from this week's readings? Why?

- What Bible verse gave you an aha moment? Share the Bible verse and what your insight is.

- What principle from this study do you want to implement more in your own life?

Discussion Questions

- Have you experienced a time when God provided joy through his Word? How did God make it real to you?

- Are there any instructions in God's Word that cause you to bristle or resist? Do you have a tendency to ignore it, explain it away, or rebel? Or do you yield—minus the joy? Is there a way to embrace the instruction in a more positive way?

- What's one thing you are seeking God's direction or discernment on right now? Explain. How will receiving the answer be a source of joy for you?

- What is your number one joy zapper? How can you counteract the zapper when it pops into your life and tries to sabotage you?

- Other than when you are spreading the gospel message, how might people recognize Christ reflected in you and want to know about the hope that lives inside you? How do you prioritize your pursuit of joy, since others are less likely to ask you about your hope when joy is absent? What about when you don't feel like pursuing joy?

- Can you think of people who have contagious joy? What are their secrets? (If you aren't sure, ask them, and also thank them for spreading joyfulness.)
- Is it possible to experience joy in the midst of suffering and trials? Obviously, circumstances cannot be the source for such joy—so what is?

Bible Verse

We ask God to give you complete knowledge of his will and to give you spiritual wisdom and understanding. Then the way you live will always honor and please the Lord, and your lives will produce every kind of good fruit. All the while, you will grow as you learn to know God better and better. We also pray that you will be strengthened with all his glorious power so you will have all the endurance and patience you need. May you be filled with joy, always thanking the Father. (Colossians 1: 9b-12a)

Assignment

Read chapters 3 and 4 before the group's next meeting. Answer the questions as you go along to enhance your individual study and to prepare to participate in the group time.

Grin Gal Pal Time

Allow time before dismissal for Grin Gal Pals to meet together. (See Week One.)

Closing Prayer

Father, we thank you for your Word, which gives us direction so we can experience the joy of following you. Help us have the discernment we need to recognize the joy zappers in our lives, and the ability to quit giving them power to ruin our days. Instead, may we be infected by joy so contagious we spread it to others. Encourage us in your Word and allow us to be refreshing to those we come in contact with this week. In Jesus' name, amen.

WEEK *Three*

Mixer

- What story stands out to you the most from this week's readings? Why?
- What Bible verse gave you an aha moment? Share the Bible verse and what your insight is.
- What principle from this study do you want to implement more in your own life?

Discussion Questions

- What is the gospel message, in a nutshell?
- If you have experienced the joy of the gospel, describe it. If you haven't yet accepted Jesus' gift of salvation, think about the reasons why. What would be one good reason to accept his gift?
- What do you think is different about the joy we have here on earth compared to the joy we will have in heaven?
- We've all heard of parties that got out of hand in a negative way, but can you think of an event where the celebration showcased the joy of the Lord? When people left the party, what was the emotion they took with them?
- You can make an ordinary day a celebration by concentrating on the amazing good things the Lord has done for you. What are some of the big and small blessings you've experienced in the last month?

- Some claim to be glass-half-full or glass-half-empty sort of people. We tend to be wired to look at life with either optimism or pessimism. How are you wired? What can you do differently to increase your level of joy?

Bible Verse

We ask God to give you complete knowledge of his will and to give you spiritual wisdom and understanding. Then the way you live will always honor and please the Lord, and your lives will produce every kind of good fruit. All the while, you will grow as you learn to know God better and better. We also pray that you will be strengthened with all his glorious power so you will have all the endurance and patience you need. May you be filled with joy, always thanking the Father. (Colossians 1: 9b-12a)

Assignment

Read chapters 5, 6, and 7 before the group's next meeting. Answer the questions as you go along to enhance your individual study and to prepare to participate in the group time.

Grin Gal Pal Time

Allow time before dismissal for Grin Gal Pals to meet together. (See Week One.)

Closing Prayer

Father, thank you for sending Jesus to our world so that we might have great joy. Help us to remember the joy of first coming to faith in you so we can share that same gospel message to others. Remind us that Jesus' work didn't end at the cross, but continues even today, in each of us. May we slow down enough to celebrate the blessings from the Giver of all good gifts. You have done amazing things! In Jesus' name, amen.

LEADER'S GUIDE

WEEK *Four*

Mixer

- What story stands out to you the most from this week's readings? Why?
- What Bible verse gave you an aha moment? Share the Bible verse and what your insight is.
- What principle from this study do you want to implement more in your own life?

Discussion Questions

- Think of a time when you forgave someone who "did you wrong." Describe the joy you experienced from being free of the hurt and pain after you forgave them.
- Have you ever been forgiven by someone else when you messed up and you knew you didn't deserve forgiveness? What did their gift of forgiveness mean to you?
- Have you ever viewed God as your Rescuer? What did he rescue you from?
- Jesus plays the role of Ransom. What price did he pay to buy you back?
- The Holy Spirit is our Refuge—our Comforter. Have you ever felt like running away from life? What does God offer in the way of refuge? Add to the list: protection, reassurance…
- Think of a time this past week when you've needed more wisdom. What did you do about it?
- How do you think joy and wisdom go hand in hand?
- What is one action step from Chapter 7 that you want to implement this coming week so you don't feel stuck or paralyzed the next time you need more wisdom?

Bible Verse

We ask God to give you complete knowledge of his will and to give you spiritual wisdom and understanding. Then the way you live will always honor and please the Lord, and your lives will produce every kind of good fruit. All the while, you will grow as you learn to know God better and better. We also pray that you will be strengthened with all his glorious power so you will have all the endurance and patience you need. May you be filled with joy, always thanking the Father. (Colossians 1: 9b-12a)

Assignment

Read chapters 8 and 9 before the group's next meeting. Answer the questions as you go along to enhance your individual study and to prepare to participate in the group time.

Grin Gal Pal Time

Allow time before dismissal for Grin Gal Pals to meet together. (See Week One.)

Closing Prayer

Blessed Father, it seems odd to start off a prayer about joy thanking you for your correction in our lives, but we are grateful for how you shape us. It blows our minds that you are interested in us, and you're an active part of creating joy in our lives. You aren't a distant spectator. We take our refuge in you and seek your renewal so we might have the energy to keep going. We're grateful for the gift of wisdom, helping us understand your truths in a way that produces growing joy. We rejoice that you delight in us! In Jesus' name, amen.

LEADER'S GUIDE

WEEK *Five*

Mixer

- What story stands out to you the most from this week's readings? Why?
- What Bible verse gave you an aha moment? Share the Bible verse and what your insight is.
- What principle from this study do you want to implement more in your own life?

Discussion Questions

- Discuss what being full of joy, or *fullness of joy*, feels like.
- If being filled with joy begins with being filled with the Spirit, is there anything you need to subtract or add to your life to pursue a Spirit-filled and joy-filled life?
- How might a change in your perspective change your joy level?
- Why do you think music is such an important part of joy?
- What can you do to insert more music into your day?
- Is there anything you can add to your Sunday worship to get more joy out of the group experience?

Bible Verse

We ask God to give you complete knowledge of his will and to give you spiritual wisdom and understanding. Then the way you live will always honor and please the Lord, and your lives will produce every kind of good fruit. All the while, you will grow as you learn to know God better and better. We also pray that you will be strengthened with all his glorious power so you will have all the endurance and patience you need. May you be filled with joy, always thanking the Father. (Colossians 1: 9b-12a)

Assignment

Read chapters 10 and 11 before the group's next meeting. Answer the questions as you go along to enhance your individual study and to prepare to participate in the group time.

Grin Gal Pal Time

Allow time before dismissal for Grin Gal Pals to meet together. (See Week One.)

Closing Prayer

Dear Joy-filler, we yield our lives in surrender and worship you. As we think of your great works and awesome attributes, we want to take time to simply adore you. May you fill our hearts with songs of joy as we praise your name. We declare you Lord, making you first place in our lives. Because of Jesus and for his glory, amen.

LEADER'S GUIDE

WEEK *Six*

Mixer

- What story stands out to you the most from this week's readings? Why?
- What Bible verse gave you an aha moment? Share the Bible verse and what your insight is.
- What principle from this study do you want to implement more in your own life?

Discussion Questions

- What does the word *endure* mean to you?
- What has been the most difficult trial for you to endure?
- How does patience influence your ability to experience joy?
- Share a time when you experienced a supernatural joy during a terrible time in your life.
- Name someone in whom you've observed joy even in trials. What can we learn from him or her?
- Think of a momentous time you cried tears of joy. What was the experience like for you?
- Remember a time when you cried mournful tears to the point of caterwauling. What prompted such a drastic response? Did you find comfort or did the sorrow linger?
- What comfort is it to know that God cares about your tears and longs to exchange your sorrow for joy?

Bible Verse

We ask God to give you complete knowledge of his will and to give you spiritual wisdom and understanding. Then the way you live will always honor and please the Lord, and your lives will produce every kind of good fruit. All the while, you will grow as you learn to know God better and better. We also pray that you will be strengthened with all his glorious power so you will have all the endurance and patience you need. May you be filled with joy, always thanking the Father. (Colossians 1: 9b-12a)

Assignment

1. Read chapters 12, 13, and the conclusion before the group's next meeting. Answer the questions as you go along to enhance your individual study and to prepare to participate in the group time.
2. Look back through the study and select your two favorite joy-filled Bible verses from the entire book. You will be asked to share one with the group.

Grin Gal Pal Time

Allow time before dismissal for Grin Gal Pals to meet together. (See Week One.)

Closing Prayer

Father, endow us with enduring joy, enough to power us through the trials we're facing. As we abide in Christ, equip us with patience—knowing you will create the ending that best fits your purpose. Help us continue to seek and serve you while we wait, even though we'd rather get a green light to leave behind our current delays. Our painful history challenges our joy, and even induces tears of grief. We look to you to deliver a joy that doesn't make sense, considering our current circumstances. May the level of our joy match the hope of our anticipated future rather than the disappointment of today's difficult situation. In Jesus' mighty name, amen.

WEEK *Seven*

Mixer

- What story stands out to you the most from this week's readings? Why?
- What Bible verse gave you an aha moment? Share the Bible verse and what your insight is.
- What principle from this study do you want to implement more in your own life?

Discussion Questions

- How can you have more strength from the Lord?
- What one thing do you need to do differently to set your mind on your faith walk?
- Go back to *Grow with Joy* in Chapter 12 and share all the benefits of joy you marked. Which one of these do you need more of in your life?
- What is your weak spot when it comes to something or someone trying to steal your joy?
- How can you shore up that weakness with God's reinforcements so you can stand against the tricks of the enemy?
- What sort of mental or spiritual exercise might help you to experience the magnitude of God's overwhelming abundance of joy in your life?
- What can you do to function with an abundance of joy, so you operate out of the overflow and avoid becoming depleted or burned out?

Bible Verse

We ask God to give you complete knowledge of his will and to give you spiritual wisdom and understanding. Then the way you live will always honor and please the Lord, and your lives will produce every kind of good fruit. All the while, you will grow as you learn to know God better and better. We also pray that you will be strengthened with all his glorious power so you will have all the endurance and patience you need. May you be filled with joy, always thanking the Father. (Colossians 1: 9b-12a)

Conclusion

Divide into smaller groups if the entire group is too large to manage these exercises in the time allotted.

Ask each woman to share her favorite joy verse from the study. They were instructed to bring two verses with them, so if one verse is chosen by someone else first, have the attendee read her second choice, to limit repetition. Ask each woman to explain why the verse means so much to her now that she's learned and processed the insights from this study.

Lead the group in setting joy goals and close the group in prayer, committing these goals to the Lord, for his glory.

Closing Prayer

Thank you, Lord, for blessing us with so many benefits of joy. There is an abundant supply, enough for us all. Even though we're finishing this study, help us be alert to the fingerprints of your joy wherever we look. And may we continue to grin, grow, go and give with joy. In the name of Jesus, amen.

Acknowledgements

There are many to whom I owe heartfelt gratitude because of their part in my writing journey. They each are responsible for helping me develop not only this book on joy, but my personal joy quotient. I'm sending grateful gratitudes to the following people and places:

Mom (Wanona Lamb Carlton). Thank you for sharing your love for the written word. When I look at my stack of books to be read, I flashback to all the times you walked us to the public library. You taught me how to grin despite the circumstances and that having a sense of humor helps too!

Patricia Rubemeyer Lewis, childhood friend. She passed away after I wrote this book, so she didn't get to see the story I wrote of our childhood friendship in the introduction. I'm thankful she brought so much joy to my early years. We played dolls, learned the facts of life, and chatted about boyfriends together.

My wisdom team. You support me with your notes, calls, prayers, and wise words. Special acknowledgement goes to Jessica Caudill, Erin Eddings, Sally Ferguson, Stephenie Hovland, Michelle Rayburn, Laurie Ritchel, Joanie Shawhan, Robin Steinweg, Gina Stinson, Leisa Stokes and Sarah Wisor.

My editors, Robin Steinweg, Rick Steele, Diane Stortz and Leisa Stokes. Thanks for polishing my words and making them shine.

My faith family at Praise Church, especially the **Willis Small Group** and my **Faith & Friends Book Club**. Life wouldn't be the same without the grins you bring to my face, but more importantly, to my heart.

Joy Weese Moll, my writing buddy. Thanks for giving me the accountability I needed to stay focused on finishing this book. How fun to put "Writing with Joy" on my calendar while writing *The Grin Gal's Guide to Joy*.

Brenham First Baptist Church for hosting a *Grin with Joy* focus group. This special group of ladies followed me through every page of this project and interacted with the material so I could make sure it worked. But more than that, you became invested in the project and cheered me on.

WordGirls. When I think of one of my favorite joy bursts, it's working in this community of writers. What great joy I gain from coaching you in your own writing endeavors!

My book designer, Michelle Rayburn. Thank you for bringing a big grin to my face with the design of this cover as well as the internal design. My book baby is a beauty, thanks to you!

My beloved husband, Russ. Nothing sparks me more than when our eyes meet and your smile lights up the room. Thanks for faithfully supporting my writing journey. Our many grin-with-joy experiences inspired this book. You make me laugh—my favorite sound—every day of our marriage.

Jesus Christ my Savior and Lord. Thank you for splashing your joy on every page of this book and, more important, in my life. May *The Grin Gal's Guide to Joy* glorify you and help your followers continue to grin, grow, go, and give with your joy.

About the Author

God's Grin Gal, Kathy Carlton Willis, writes and speaks with a balance of funny and faith, whimsy and wisdom. She coaches others to remove the training wheels of fear and not just risk, but also take pleasure in the joy ride of life. She is known for her debut book, *Grin with Grace* and for her grinning Boston Terrier, Hettie.

Not many funny girls also have Bible degrees! She graduated with honors from Bible College, holding degrees in Bible and Church Education, and has served for thirty years in full-time church ministry with her pastor/husband, Russ. She's active as a book industry pro, while also staying involved in her church.

Kathy works with women's groups and writers' groups, inside and outside the church. She's passionate about helping believers have "aha! moments" with the daily application of Scripture.

Even with all the circumstances she's faced, she gives a very clear message that she possesses an expectant hope and contentment in the Lord. Something we can all experience.

Kathy Carlton Willis owns KCW Communications, spinning many plates as writer, editor, speaker, and coach. Over 1,000 of her writing projects have appeared online and in print publications.

CBN.com features Kathy's popular blog. Their website consistently ranks among the top 10 most popular sites in the Lifestyle—Religion category. *Grin & Grow with Kathy* offers a twice-monthly devo-study utilizing her story, study, and steps format.

She is a contributing writer for *The Christian Communicator, Upgrade Your Life, The Christian Pulse*, along with others. Kathy also writes inspirational, motivational and transparent posts on social media.

Kathy founded WordGirls, a community of Christian female writers who receive professional coaching from Kathy.

She writes and speaks on the issues that hold believers back and shines the light on their path to freedom. Kathy shines, whether she's shining the light on God's writers and speakers, or reflecting God's light during her speaking opportunities.

Learn more at Kathy's website: **kathycarltonwillis.com**

3G Books

In addition to *The Grin Gal's Guide to Joy*, Kathy Carlton Willis has started a line of books designed to release two to three times per year. Kathy's boldly practical tips, tools, and takeaways show up in Christian living books, Bible studies, and devo-studies. 3G Books are perfect for small groups or individual reading. Look for her next book later in 2020.

The first book to kick off 3G Books was created with speakers in mind.

Packed cover-to-cover with invaluable information, *The Ultimate Speaker's Guide* is the new bible for communicators. With almost two decades of industry knowledge under her belt, Kathy Carlton Willis has coached hundreds of speakers to help them develop successful speaking businesses. This book covers all the tips, tools, and takeaways you'll need to ensure that your audience increases and your message is heard, including:

- Setting up your business
- Finding a brand that fits
- Getting more bookings
- Polishing your style
- Discovering God's plan for your business

An extensive resource section containing a sample contract, media interviewing tips, fee schedules, checklists, and much more, makes *The Ultimate Speaker's Guide* an essential toolkit you'll use time and again.

Praise for *The Ultimate Speaker's Guide*:

"Whether you're new to speaking to promote the message God has given you or have been doing it for a while, you'll find a wealth of practical help in *The Ultimate Speaker's Guide*. Kathy's experience as a speaker and trainer fills a void in resources for Christian speakers."

—Lin Johnson, Write-to-Publish Conference Director Managing Editor of *Christian Communicator*

Buy the Book at Amazon www.amazon.com/dp/1733072802

www.ingramcontent.com/pod-product-compliance
Lightning Source LLC
Chambersburg PA
CBHW080542090426
42734CB00016B/3184